A Paperback Original
First published 1990 by
Poolbeg Press Ltd
Knocksedan House
Swords Co Dublin Ireland

© Art Byrne and Sean McMahon 1990

Reprinted July, 1994

ISBN 1 85371 094 6

Cover painting by Pomphrey Associates
Illustrations by John Short
Set by Richard Parfrey in Palatino 10/14
Printed by The Guernsey Press Co. Ltd
Vale Guernsey Channel Islands

Lives

113 Great
Irishwomen
and Irishmen

by Art Byrne and Sean McMahon

POOLBEG

For our kind but exacting editor,
Jo O'Donoghue

CONTENTS

A Note on the Text

Names occurring in the text that are marked with an
asterisk are the subject of a separate entry

INTRODUCTION

Who fed the Abbey actors with Gort cake? What Clareman invented the submarine? What beautiful Sligo girl was a crack shot and married a Polish count? What saint was said to have started a war over a book he copied? What songwriter used to draw pictures on white plates with a lighted candle? What bishop is supposed to have filled vacant parishes in his diocese by having the eligible curates run races?

The answers to these questions and to many others may be found in this book of Irish lives. For more than 2000 years of history, many of them troubled, many of them black, the "indomitable Irishry" have made their mark and in that time this small green country has produced more than its share of colourful characters. From the thousands of Irish women and men who have a claim to our attention because of what they did or said or wrote we have chosen a baker's dozen over the hundred and given brief accounts of their careers. Not all of them are noble or heroic though there are a fair number of saints; some, indeed, could be said to be downright wicked, including one pair of murderers who are a disgrace to their decent Irish names. All are guaranteed Irish and guaranteed interesting.

The names are arranged in alphabetical order for convenience of consultation but the book is not meant to be just a reference book. It's a book to pick up and enjoy when you have a minute or two to spare. The drawings will give you some idea of what the people looked like and the entries will tell you the interesting things about their lives.

THE HYMN LADY

Cecil Frances Alexander (1818-95)

At this very moment, somewhere in the world, a school choir is singing "All Things Bright and Beautiful"; and every Christmas, wherever carols are sung, you will hear "Once in Royal David's City." The lady who wrote these famous hymns was born in Wicklow but her father, Major Humphreys, became land steward to the Duke of Abercorn when she was fifteen so she grew up in Strabane, Co Tyrone. She taught Sunday School in the town and finding that the hymns which the children had to sing were too dull and too hard, decided to write more suitable ones herself. They appeared in a little book called *Verses for the Holy Seasons* (1848) where "All Things" was originally called "Septuagesima" and the carol entitled "Christmas." In 1850 at the late age (for those days) of thirty she married William Alexander, a curate who was six years younger than she. They lived in different parts of the Derry diocese, including West Tyrone and Fahan, until finally William became bishop. Their house on the city walls looked across at the hill of Creggan which was the inspiration for her third famous hymn, "There Is a Green Hill Far Away," which has as second line the words, "Without a city wall." The great French composer, Charles Gounod, thought it the most perfect hymn ever written and wrote special music for it. Cecil Alexander died in Derry on 12 October 1895 and was the first Protestant to be buried in the city cemetery with a cross for a memorial. Her three most famous hymns are reproduced in stained glass windows in the baptistry of Derry Cathedral.

THE DESERT GENERAL

H R L G Alexander (1891-1969)

To the soldiers who served under him he was "Alex," the tall thin moustached general who unusually for a commander spent more time at the front-line than back in headquarters. To the aristocratic world into which he was born, he was Harold Rupert Leofric George, third son of the earl of Caledon, whose seat was in Co Tyrone. As expected, he went to Harrow, to Sandhurst and then joined the Irish Guards. He married, suitably, Lady Margaret Bingham. He had not intended to be a career soldier but his record during the 1914-18 war which he began as a lieutenant and finished as a brigade commander and during which he was twice decorated suggested that soldiering was where his abilities lay. He saw service in Latvia in 1919 and on the Indian frontier, and he was the youngest general in the army on the outbreak of war in 1939. He had the misfortune to be involved in the retreats from Dunkirk and Burma so he was lucky that Churchill allowed him a final chance in north Africa. There under the supreme command of Eisenhower, he defeated the German-Italian force at Tunis and went on to command the invasion of Sicily and Italy. It must have been disappointing to him that the Italian front became secondary to the Normandy and Russian fronts, which meant he could fight only a holding campaign with limited forces, commanding what were unfairly called the "D-day dodgers." He finished the war a field-marshal and went to Canada as British governor-general. His final job was as a not-too-happy minister of defence (1952-54) in the post-war government of Winston Churchill. It was a period when no British minister of defence could have been very happy. He died Earl Alexander of Tunis on 16 June 1969.

THE ABBEY SISTERS

Molly (1887-1952) and Sara (1883-1950) Allgood

The history of the Abbey Theatre has been told many times but many people do not know that the careers of the first Pegeen Mike and the first Juno ended in Hollywood with these fine actresses playing minor parts in undistinguished films. Molly Allgood, who used the stage name Maire O'Neill, joined the company a year after her older sister Sara had appeared in the first play ever presented in the theatre (as Mrs Fallon in Lady Gregory's play, *Spreading the News*). John Synge,* the greatest of the Abbey playwrights, fell in love with Molly and he certainly had her in mind when he wrote the part of Pegeen Mike in *The Playboy of the Western World* and the posthumously staged *Deirdre of the Sorrows*. He died in 1909 and two years later she married G H Mair, the drama critic of the *Manchester Guardian*. They had two children, Pegeen and John and when her husband died in 1926 Molly married an old friend from the Abbey, Arthur Sinclair. They had a successful theatrical partnership but the marriage ended in divorce. Molly in the end made a tolerable living playing small parts in films. She died on 2 January 1952.

After her Abbey debut Sara worked for ten years with the company and then went on a world tour with *Peg O'My Heart*, a famous and very popular light comedy. She married her leading man, Gerald Henson, in 1916 but both he and their only child died in 1918. She returned to the Abbey and had triumphs as Juno in the Sean O'Casey play *Juno and the Paycock* (1924) and as Bessie Burgess in *The Plough and the Stars* (1926). She made a number of films for Alfred Hitchcock including *Blackmail* and the film versions of *Juno* and *Riders to the Sea*. She settled in Hollywood in 1940 and appeared in thirty films. She died in poverty on 13 September 1950.

THE CUSTOMS OFFICER WHO BELIEVED IN FAIRIES

William Allingham (1824-99)

Why daren't we go a-hunting up the airy mountain and down the rushy glen? How many ducks were there on that pond with the green bank beyond? Most people know the answers to those trivial questions, but how many know that the author, who came from Ballyshannon, Co Donegal was for twenty-four years a customs officer? William Allingham was born on the 19 March 1824, the son of a merchant. His mother died when he was nine. He wanted to be a poet and in time he became a close friend of

Tennyson and a member of the Pre-Raphaelite Brother-hood, a group of lively young men who wished to change the way artists painted. He was not happy at school and his father found him a job in a bank when he was fifteen. He did not like this much either but he found the customs service more to his taste. During these working years he wrote lots of poetry but he was too shy to admit it. Instead he had it printed on broadsheets and was happy to watch pedlars at fairs selling such poems as "Lovely Mary Donnelly" and "Adieu to Belashanny" (a pronounciation nearer to the Irish name of the town) while no one knew that he was the author. "The Fairies," his best-known poem, was written in Killybegs when he was on a tour of duty. When he left the service he went to England. He became editor of *Fraser's Magazine* in 1870. He married Helen Patterson, a water-colourist twenty-four years his junior, and had a most happy married life. He died on 18 November 1899 and is buried in Ballyshannon.

THE MAN WITH THE BIG RED BOOK

Eamonn Andrews (1922-85)

He might be dressed as a commissionaire, or an ambulance driver, or he would step from behind a curtain, the last person his quarry expected; or sometimes in a double bluff the willing decoy would turn out to be the one he was after. Soon, however, there would be the brilliant, lop-sided smile, the big red book and the most famous Irish voice of all, saying, "XY, you thought you were here to...but tonight XY, This is Your Life" and another public and very accelerated biography would be disclosed in one of the most popular television series ever. A fellow Irishman,

Danny Blanchflower, was the only one ever to refuse to perform—a tribute to the accolade conveyed by selection and the reassurance of the genial presenter's personality.

Eamonn Andrews was born on 19 December 1922 in Synge Street, Dublin, the son of hardworking, respectable parents. He was a good boxer, a studious pupil, had early ambitions as a writer and actually wrote a not very successful play called *The Moon is Black*. He left a steady job selling insurance to be a full-time broadcaster. He worked with Radio Éireann as compère and boxing-commentator and in the Theatre Royal as question-master of the Double or Nothing Quiz. Finally he became chairman of a zany comedy show, *Ignorance is Bliss*, with the BBC in 1950 and his career was fully launched. He became extremely busy doing sports and children's programmes and broke into television with the game show *What's My Line*, which made his boxer's face familiar to millions of Sunday night viewers throughout the fifties. His greatest success was with *This Is Your Life* which began on 29 July 1955 with Eamonn as the first subject. The show ran until 1961 and then he joined ITV to host one of Britain's first chat-shows. *This Is Your Life* was revived in 1969 and continued until Eamonn's death on 4 November 1985 of muscular deterioration of the heart. He was made a Knight of St Gregory in 1964 and received the OBE in 1970.

THE PROTESTANT RADICAL

James Brown Armour (1841-1928)

It takes courage to swim against the tide of a general belief.
In the Ulster of the 1890s most Protestants believed that
home (self-)rule for Ireland would end in economic disaster
and a loss of religious freedom. Armour, the leader of those
who refused this argument, was born in Ballymoney, Co
Antrim, on 20 January 1841, educated at the Royal Belfast
Academical Institution and the Queen's Colleges of Belfast
and Cork. As a Presbyterian minister in his native town he
supported the local tenant-farmers in their struggle with
landlords for fairer rents. At Senate in the university in

Belfast he argued for the teaching of Irish and scholastic philosophy so as to encourage the enrolment of Catholic students. Above all at meetings of the Presbyterian general assembly he continually criticised his church for its support of unionism. True, his argument was rather negative: he felt that Presbyterians could not possibly do worse under a Catholic-majority home rule than under a Church of Ireland-dominated union. He was not of the romantic tradition that believed independence would cure all Ireland's problems. Yet, across a gap of almost a century, the words he spoke at May Street Presbyterian Church in Belfast in March 1893 touch a chord: "This assembly will be known as the assembly which, in its unreasoning passion against Mr Gladstone and to spite the majority of our fellow-countrymen, sold its people into bondage, and through a senseless fear of Romanism, sacrificed the power and progress of true Presbyterianism in Ireland for generations." In later years he was to find the Ulster Volunteers of the 1912 gun-running and the Irish volunteers of the 1916 uprising equally repellent. He lived out his life in Ballymoney, secure in a happy marriage and a congregation that never deserted him. "Armour of Ballymoney" died on 25 January 1928.

THE FATHER OF NOBODY'S CHILDREN

Thomas John Barnardo (1845-1905)

Nowadays Eastenders seem quite a happy lot, but in the last century in London's East End, thousands of children, some orphans but many more simply abandoned by their parents, were hungry, homeless and sick. Many died while they were still young but those who survived had no education or training. Kind-hearted people who walked the streets of the gas-lit foggy city and saw these poor homeless creatures must have wondered why no one did anything about their plight. These were the days before government benefits; the only hope was that good people would help them voluntarily. One young medical student, seeing the situation, decided that he at least would do what he could.

His name was Thomas John Barnardo and he was born in Dublin on 4 July 1845, the son of a furrier. He attended a Protestant revivalist meeting when he was seventeen and was converted. He began his work for souls in Dublin but soon decided to become a missionary to China and determined to become a doctor because he thought that a medical degree would be useful in his work. It was when he was at medical school in London that he realised that charity began at home in the East End. He opened his first home for destitute boys in 1870 and established a girl's village in 1874. By 1900 the homes he had opened sheltered 6000 boys and in general lived up to his own rule that "No destitute child should ever be turned away." One of his pamphlets was called *The Rescue of the Waif.* By the time of his death on 19 September 1905 he knew he had rescued 250,000 children.

THE FATHER OF THE AMERICAN NAVY

John Barry (1745-1803)

On Wexford's Crescent Quay stands a statue of a naval
figure by the American sculptor Wheeler Williams. He is
dressed as all service-men were in those days in ordinary
clothes: cloak, frock coat and breeches, fore-and-aft hat, and
high boots. The inscription says: *John Barry, Father of the
American Navy.* He was born in Tacumshane, Co Wexford,
about 1745, but left Ireland when quite young to go to sea as
a deck-hand or a cabin-boy. He made his home in
Pennsylvania. By 1760 he was a master mariner, trading
with the West Indies. In 1775 the American War of

Independence began and all masters who supported the rebel cause became warship captains though their ships were merely converted merchantmen. Barry's own ship, the *Black Prince*, became the *Alfred*. In 1776 after the American colonies had declared themselves independent, Barry as captain of the warship *Lexington* made the first maritime capture of the war when the British ship *Edward* was taken to Philadelphia as a prize. After many vicissitudes due to his quick temper and the lack of resources of the Continental Congress which ran the war, he was again given a command, this time of the *Alliance* in 1781. He was sent on a mission to France, America's ally in the war, carrying one of George Washington's senior officers. The mission was successful but he had to deal with mutinies on the way out and on the way back. He quelled them both and captured two British ships on the voyage home though he was severely wounded in the fighting. After the war he left the sea, the American congress having decided that a standing navy was unnecessary in peacetime. He continued to agitate for the establishment of a permanent navy and finally persuaded the government under President Adams to build three ships. His last years were spent in organising the navy and earning the title that is engraved on the pedestal of his statue. He died on 13 September 1803.

EN ATTENDANT

Samuel Beckett (1906-89)

One of the literary ironies of the post-war years was that some of the most beautiful English prose was produced by an Irishman translating his own French originals. Samuel Beckett was born on Good Friday, 13 April 1906, in Foxrock at the foot of the Dublin mountains, of a well-off, sports-loving father and a devout Church of Ireland mother. Both landscape and parental relationship strongly influenced his later writing. After school at Portora, Enniskillen, he was a brilliant student of modern languages at Trinity, before going to lecture in Paris where he wrote on Proust and became a close friend of Joyce.* During the 1930s he moved restlessly between Dublin, London and Germany, published poems and a novel which had little success, and finally settled in Paris where he married Suzanne Dumesnil. He chose to remain in France when war broke out, worked with the *maquis* in resisting the German occupation, and at the end of the war began to write in French. Recognition finally came in 1951 when *Molloy*, a depiction of life's hopelessness written in a spare but very funny prose, was acclaimed by the Parisian intellectual élite. A much more popular success was *En Attendant Godot*, the absurdly funny play about two garrulous tramps to whom "nothing happens, twice." Beckett continued to write in the same vein but more and more tersely. He shunned publicity, refused to attend the prize-giving ceremony when he was awarded the Nobel prize in 1969, and never allowed himself to be filmed or tape-recorded. In this way he forced people to approach him through his writings, to the extent that when he died on 22 December 1989 he was remembered on television with readings from *Premier Amour*, in *The Irish Times* with a poem, and in *L'Humanité* with the headline "Godot n'attend plus Samuel Beckett."

FEAR AN BHIOBLA

William Bedell (1571-1642)

Few cities are as dominated by a university campus as Dublin is by Trinity College. It forces the city's main thoroughfare to deviate southwards; one needs to study an aerial photograph to realise what an enormous area (at least fifty acres) of the city centre is covered by the college grounds. To walk the campus is to marvel at the buildings of four different centuries, at the intimate squares and the green open spaces.

The college was founded to extend English civilisation and English control in Ireland in 1591. Naturally the early provosts were recruited in England. Of Essex yeoman stock, William Bedell had been a fellow of a Cambridge college, a secretary to the British ambassador to Venice, and rector of a parish, before he came to Ireland in 1627. As provost of Trinity, he is remembered for rewriting the statutes governing the college, for forcing the families of deceased provosts to pay outstanding debts to the college, and above all for encouraging Church of Ireland ordinands to learn Irish and for supervising a translation of the Bible into the native language.

Later he became Bishop of Kilmore where he was to die of a fever caught while ministering to refugees from the war which began in Ulster in 1641. The O'Reillys, who had captured him, paid him military honours at his funeral. Perhaps they appreciated the qualities of the tough-minded Puritan from England better than did his academic colleagues who took until 1685 to publish *Bedell's Bible*. (By this time, the native Irish were seen as being confirmed in their Catholicism and unlikely to be won over to the reformed faith.)

"ESSE EST AUT PERCIPI AUT PERCIPERE"

George Berkeley (1685-1753)

One of the eighteenth-century philosophers who continue to influence contemporary thought, Berkeley was born in Co Kilkenny on 12 March 1685. He was successively student, fellow and tutor at Trinity, and while there he wrote his first book *The Principles of Human Knowledge* (1710). Having spent a number of years in France and Italy he became dean of Derry in 1724. Four years later he went to America where he planned a college to educate both colonist and native. His plan came to nothing and he returned to Ireland to become bishop of Cloyne. There he became interested in social and economic problems and he wrote on them in *The Querist*. Finally ill-health forced him to resign and move to Oxford where he died in January 1753.

To summarise the beliefs of a philosopher, and particularly of Berkeley, is to betray them. Better to give some of his own words: "The table I write on I say exists; that is, I see and feel it: and if I were out of my study I should say it existed; meaning thereby that if I was in my study I might perceive it. There was an odour, that is, it was smelt; there was a sound, that is, it was heard; a colour or figure, and it was perceived by sight or touch. This is all I can understand by these and the like expressions. For as to what is said of the 'absolute' existence of unthinking things, without any relation to their being perceived, that is to me perfectly unintelligible. Their *esse* is *percipi*; nor is it possible they should have any existence out of the minds or thinking things which perceive them."

"BRIAN COONEY"

Charles Bianconi (1786-1875)

It takes the average car driver three-and-a-half hours to
drive from Derry to Dublin. In 1800 it took nearly as many
days. Roads were poor and the world of the ordinary people
of Ireland was bounded by the distance they could walk. All
this was changed in July 1815 when the first "bian" carrying
the mail ran between Clonmel and Cahir. The journey took
less than two hours and cost one shilling and eightpence,
making it much cheaper than the stage coach and much
faster than the canal barge. The bian was an open two-
wheeler car which carried six passengers, three a side, and

the driver. Its name came from the young Italian who saw that Ireland needed a fast, cheap transport system and set out to supply one.

Charles Bianconi was born in the north of Italy on 2 September 1786 and came to Ireland first as a seller of prints and mirrors. He set up a shop in Clonmel and did well. His Tipperary customers called him Brian Cooney, which was the nearest Irish sound they could get to his Italian name. When the wars with Napoleon ended in 1815 there were many ex-war horses for sale and soon bians were running on many roads in the south-west of the country. By 1835 the crimson and yellow cars with their silver harness were well known in Munster, Leinster and Connacht. Bianconi was a devout Catholic, a friend of Daniel O'Connell* and Fr Mathew* (who had once rescued him from an attack in the street.) In 1825 bians brought many of O'Connell's supporters to an important election. By 1843 bians were covering 4000 miles a day and the astute owner was buying shares in Dargan*'s railways. In 1846 he bought a large house and estate at Longfield near Cashel and did much relief work during the Famine. He sold his business to his employees on good terms and spent the last years of his life still rich, and active in politics. They say the sound of horses' hooves were heard outside the house when he died on 22 September 1875.

THE KING WHO WAS NO SAINT

Brian Boru (c. 941-1014)

There was once a king called Brian Boru. He was born in Thomond in 914 and became King of Munster in 978. You have surely seen his picture with a gold crown on his head, kneeling before a crucifix in his tent, too old to fight in his last and greatest battle against the Scandinavian invaders at Clontarf on Good Friday in the year 1014. You may even have seen the painting of the Norse warrior, Brodir, with his broadsword held aloft over the frail neck about to slay this great High-King who had done so much for his land. Brian Boru had united the country, persuaded the local chieftains to accept him as Ard Rí, reformed the Church, brought prosperity and with the success of the battle driven the foreigner out of Ireland for good.

It is a great story and why not? It was written by experts, a few centuries after Clontarf. The O'Brien clan needed publicity so they brought in the best copywriters of the day, *na filí*, to write the best possible account. The particular *file* who wrote Brian's story put it in a book called *Cogadh Gaedhil re Gallaibh*. In fact it was not a war between Irish and foreigners but one between Brian and his Munstermen and the men of Leinster. The Norsemen who lived in Leinster lent a hand but they were not significant militarily and Brian kept up good relations with his own Norsemen who ran the ports of Limerick and Cork. As for helping the Church, as an astute politician he realised he needed all the help he could get when, as ever, the Ulster clan chiefs proved intractable. He did not need the myth-making of the *file*. His career which took him from the obscure local kingdom of Dal gCais to the final subjection of the Ulstermen was glorious enough. After Clontarf it was as "King of all the Irish" that he was buried in Armagh.

THE GAS MAN

Robert Boyle (1627-91)

Up to the middle of the seventeenth-century people believed that chemistry, which they called alchemy, was the study of how to change other metals into gold. One of the first to make a move towards the modern science of chemistry was an Irishman from Lismore, Co Waterford. He was born on 23 January 1627, the brilliant seventh son of Robert Boyle, Earl of Cork. He became a pupil at Eton at eight years of age and did the Grand Tour of Europe when he was eleven. At Florence at the age of fifteen he made a point of studying the papers of the great Galileo, who had just died. He lived in England during the Civil War and the Commonwealth and he was one of a number of scientists who met secretly in London because of government and church suspicion. When Charles II was restored to the English throne in 1660 and began to encourage the study of science, Robert became a member of the Royal Society. He was interested in pneumatics, crystallography and blood circulation. His experiments with gas-compression caused him to enunciate the physical law which is called after him: $pv=k$ (at constant temperature the product of pressure and volume is a constant.) This Boyle's Law is important in all kinds of ways; for example, it is the principle behind such things as pumping up a bicycle-tyre or the use of an oxy-acetylene torch. Boyle was the first man to distinguish between a *mixture*, where the ingredients mixed retain their original chemical properties, and a *compound*, where the result has properties not possessed by the elements which were compounded. He was also very religious; he taught himself Hebrew and Greek, not for pleasure but the better to study the Bible, and he contributed £700, a large sum of money in those days, to have the scriptures translated into Irish and distributed, by Bishop Bedell.* Although he was beset by ill-health and near-blindness he lived a long time considering the normal life-expectancy of the age, and died on the last day of 1691.

THE NAVIGATOR

St Brendan (c. 489-575)

St Brendan and his followers had sailed far out into the ocean and come to an island. They landed and started a fire to cook a meal. The island began to move. The terrified monks rushed to their boat from where they watched the island move further and further away from them. Then Brendan spoke: "Where we were was not an island but a fish—the foremost of all that swim in the ocean. He is always trying to bring his tail to meet his head but he cannot because of his length."

Such "fishy" stories made the *Navigatio Sancti Brendani*

Abbatis (c. 800), an anonymous compilation of voyage-tales, a best-seller in medieval Europe. Quiet-living Christians gave thanks for Brendan's miraculous escape from the whale. Restless sailors looked there for evidence of new lands beyond the ocean. Nor is this *immram* (as such stories were called in Irish) without use for the historian. From it we learn much about the practice of early monks, and we get the only two definite facts we have about Brendan's life. He was born near Loch Léin in Co Kerry and he founded a large monastery at Clonfert, Co Galway.

THE SAINT OF SPRING

St Brighid (?-c. 525)

If you like maps, the atlas of Ireland which the Royal Irish Academy published in 1979 is a fascinating book. There are maps that give information on every conceivable topic, from the mean water discharge of rivers to the distribution of cattle breeds. Among the most interesting are the twenty-one maps showing folk traditions. One map shows different types of cross and where they are made: a simple wooden cross in Clare; a diamond-shaped straw cross in Kerry; one of interlaced bows of straw in Sligo; commonest of all, the overlapping straw cross, made everywhere from

Cork to Antrim. What unites all of these types of crosses is the name of Brighid, in whose honour they are made. She is said to have converted a dying pagan by plaiting a cross from the rushes strewn on his hut floor. Such stories were written in hagiographies by monks who wished to turn people from old pagan customs to the new Christian belief. Thus an ancient fertility rite was changed to honour Brighid on her feast on February 1. Beyond the traditional stories we know little. She may have been born at Faughart in Co Louth and she is said to have set up a convent at Kildare. What matter, when her name has lived on through its association with a beautiful traditional art?

THE EARL BISHOP

Frederick Hervey, Fourth Earl of Bristol
(1730-1803)

On the north Irish coast between the mouths of the Roe and Bann rivers lies the magnificent Magilligan-Downhill strand. As the train from Derry travels to Coleraine it passes the strand and goes through two long tunnels before emerging at Castlerock. The passenger with a sharp eye will see on the very edge of the cliff at the first tunnel a strange building shaped like a bell-jar. This Mussenden Temple and the strand itself are part of the colourful life of Frederick Hervey, the Bishop of Derry and fourth Earl of Bristol. He

34

was born in the family house of Ickworth in Surrey on 1 August 1730 and after education at Winchester and Cambridge took holy orders. When his brother George became Lord Lieutenant of Ireland Frederick went with him as chaplain. He was given the bishopric of Cloyne and then the much richer see of Derry. There is a story that he heard the news of his translation while playing leap-frog and he announced to his friends, "I have surpassed you all; in one leap I have jumped from Cloyne to Derry."

When he was younger he had become an expert in art and architecture and used his money to build beautiful houses at Downhill and Ballyscullion. He was liberal in politics and was a colonel in the Derry regiment of the Irish Volunteers, whose existence led to the setting up of Grattan*'s parliament. He was, like Grattan, a strong supporter of Catholic emancipation. His later years were spent touring the continent seeking a cure for gout and causing many inns in European cities to be named Hotel Bristol. He died in Rome on 8 July 1803. The Mussenden Temple on the Downhill cliff near the ruin of his great house is a typical eighteenth-century rotunda and was called after his cousin Frideswide. Below it is the beach where, it is said, this quixotic aristocrat used to hold the horse- and foot-races to determine which of his curates should be promoted to parishes.

THE UNIONIST SQUIRE

Basil Brooke (1888-1973)

He was born at Colebrook, Co Fermanagh on 9 June 1888
into a family with a long and glorious tradition. (The first of
the "fighting Brookes" had been knighted by Elizabeth I).
This Brooke followed in the family tradition of education at
Winchester and Sandhurst, and then service in the 11th
Hussars. In the 1914-18 war he won the Military Cross and
the Croix de Guerre. On returning to the family estate he
served the newly-established N. Ireland by becoming
commandant of the B-Specials, an almost entirely
Protestant, part-time, armed police-force. An MP since

1929, he once assured his fellow Orangemen at a Twelfth of July celebration that he would employ no Catholics as "they are out to destroy Ulster with all their might and power." Brooke served as minister of agriculture under the aging Craig and soon after his death was prime minister in his place. He steered his province through the upset of the 1939-45 war (in which two of his sons served and died), through the post-war socialist changes imposed from Westminster, through the relative prosperity of the 1950s (when an IRA campaign failed to get Catholic support), until his retirement in the early 1960s. He was created Viscount Brookeborough in 1952. He could pride himself that after twenty years in power he left Ulster just as British, and even more prosperous than it had been before. He lived another ten years, long enough to see destroyed the might and power of the Ulster he had helped build. His death on 18 August 1973 led one who knew him to comment that those who found Brooke a charming man when relaxing away from his desk did not realise that there was no desk.

THE MUSICAL SCRIBE

Edward Bunting (1773-1843)

In the assembly rooms of the Belfast exchange all the most lively of the citizens and some visitors from outside the city are gathered. Mary Ann McCracken* is there with her brother Harry and his Dublin friend Wolfe Tone.* She waves to "Atty" Bunting, the young organist at the parish church, who lodges with the McCrackens. There is a hush in the room as Arthur O'Neill, the blind harper, begins to play "The Princess Royal." Apart from the fingers of the harper the only movement is from the pen of Bunting who is busily noting down the tune.

The young musical scribe at the Belfast festival of harpers (July 1792) was soon captivated by the patriotic ideal of preserving Ireland's ancient music. Immediately after the festival he toured Ulster to listen to musicians, from whom he collected tunes which he published in 1796 as *A General Collection of the Ancient Irish Music*. Later he visited Connacht and employed a man to take down the Irish words of the songs he had collected.

So Bunting became the first great collector of Irish traditional music. To him we owe the survival of many beautiful airs and our knowledge of the early harpers' way of playing. Unfortunately, though he copied the tunes accurately, when he came to publish them he altered notes and keys to fit his own theory of harmony. And instead of publishing the Irish words he had a versifier write new ones in English. Bunting envied Tom Moore*'s success as a writer of lyrics and so failed to see why he as a collector could not take similar liberties with traditional tunes.

Born in Armagh, he spent his later years as organist of St Stephen's in Dublin, where he married a Miss Chapman. Though he published a final collection in 1840, all his productive fieldwork had been done before the second volume of *Ancient Irish Music* was issued in 1809.

THE BODY SNATCHERS

William Burke (1792-1829)
and William Hare (?)

In Edinburgh in the middle of the nineteenth century street children used to chant the macabre rhyme:

Burke's the murd'rer, Hare's the thief
And Knox the boy who buys the beef.

It tells the story of a pair of murderous thugs who found a neat way of making money from corpses without the trouble of digging them up. Edinburgh was the leading British medical school and Dr Knox, the chief anatomist, was constantly in need of specimens for his anatomy lectures. Before the Anatomy Act of 1832 it was illegal and immoral to anatomise cadavers but Knox was prepared to pay good money for fresh material. Resurrectionists used haunt graveyards and unless the family of the deceased could afford to hire guards, the corpse of their dear departed was likely to end up on Knox's dissecting table.

William Burke was born in Urney near Strabane on the Tyrone-Donegal border in 1792. He worked as a "navigator" on the canals of Scotland and by 1827 was living with his "wife" Helen McDougal in a lodging house in Edinburgh kept by a Derryman, William Hare, of whose previous life nothing is known. Hare was tall and thin while Burke was thickset and squat. When an old lodger, a Highlander called Donald, died and Hare got £10 for the body from Dr Knox, he suggested to Burke that this was a neat way of making money without having to body-snatch. Aided by their "wives" Burke and Hare disposed of a total of sixteen people by getting them drunk and then asphyxiating them: Hare covered their mouths and noses while Burke sat on their chests and drove the air out of their lungs. Their victims were mostly derelicts, one being the mentally-retarded daughter of a previous victim, Mary Haldane. The girl had asked Hare where her mother was and he very obligingly offered to take her to join the mother. A persistent police officer called Ferguson eventually found incriminating evidence in Hare's house. Hare turned King's evidence and Burke was hanged on 28 January 1829. With fitting irony his body was ordered to be given to the anatomists. Before he died Burke exonerated Knox from all complicity. Hare is supposed to have gone south to work at a lime-kiln and to have been blinded by his fellow-workers when they discovered who he was. He died old and blind, having worked a begging-pitch outside the British Museum in London.

THE ELOQUENT VOICE OF CONSERVATISM

Edmund Burke (1729-97)

Born at 12 Arran Quay, Dublin, on 12 January 1729, the son of a solicitor and of a Catholic mother, Edmund Burke was educated at a Quaker school and at Trinity College. He went to London to study law, and, developing an interest in writing, became editor of the Annual Register and one of Dr Johnson's famous "Club." A job as private secretary to the prime minister, Lord Rockingham, led naturally to his becoming an MP in 1765. At Westminster he developed his great gifts as an eloquent and persuasive writer and speaker. As a liberal he spoke for the American colonists, even when they demanded independence from England, for the Irish Catholics when they looked for political rights and against the corrupt administration of India by Warren Hastings. Then in 1789 came the revolutionary changes in France which were welcomed by most of Burke's colleagues in the Whig party, but condemned by Burke who saw it as part of "the nature of things" that France should be governed by a king and an aristocracy. *Reflections on the Revolution in France* was first published in 1790, translated immediately into French, and became the bible of those who opposed revolutionary change. His old political friends shunned him and when he died at his house at Beaconsfield near London on 9 July 1797, he was as much an outsider as when he was born the Protestant son of a Catholic mother, or when he became a penniless MP in a parliament of wealthy landowners, or when he first addressed the English parliament with his strange Irish voice.

THE IRISH DIVA

Margaret Burke Sheridan (1889-1958)

There was once a Mayo girl who sang like an Italian and who was better than any Italian at singing Madame Butterfly in the period between the two world wars. She was born on 15 September 1889 in Castlebar, the youngest of a family of five children. Their mother died in 1893 and she was the only one who stayed at home with the father while the rest went to America. When he died in 1901 she became a permanent boarder with the Dominican sisters in Eccles Street, Dublin. It was they who discovered her marvellous lyric soprano voice. Dr Vincent O'Brien, who had taught singing to John McCormack* and James Joyce,* took her as a pupil and somehow found the money to send her for two years to the Royal Academy of Music in London. She was introduced to London society by her patrons, Lord and Lady de Walden, and became friendly with many of the public figures of the day. It was the great Marconi, the inventor of wireless telegraphy, who brought her to Italy in 1917 and arranged for further study in Rome. In 1918 she made her debut as Mimi in *La Bohème*. All during the twenties she was famous for her interpretation of Madame Butterfly. So famous did her *insuperabile* performance become that the composer Puccini came to see her and decided to coach her personally for the leading role in his opera *Manon*. As a token of his appreciation he presented her with a magnificent costume to wear in the second act. When he died of throat cancer in 1924 she was the main performer in many concerts held in his honour throughout Italy. She made frequent appearances at Covent Garden, representing La Scala, Milan, and was a worthy partner of the fiery conductor, Toscanini. In 1936, after an unhappy love-affair, she forsook the opera stage and in 1939 returned to Ireland. She was at the height of her powers when she made her sudden decision to retire. From 1939 until her death from cancer on 16 April 1958 she lived partly in America and partly in Ireland. She is buried in Glasnevin Cemetery.

THE BLIND HARPER

Turlough Carolan (1670-1738)

These are the opening bars of "Carolan's Receipt." Try them on your tin whistle and you will hear the music of a happy man. The story behind the tune is that on his way home from Tulsk Carolan called on his friend Dr John Stafford, who offered him dinner and naturally some whiskey after the meal. Carolan enjoyed the hospitality so much that he "forgot" to go home. Next morning he composed the tune for his host.

However, not all of Carolan's story is of happiness. He was born near Nobber in Co Meath but then the family moved to Roscommon, to work for the family of MacDermott Roe at Alderford. At the age of eighteen years Carolan caught the small-pox that left him blind. At the time music was one of the few avenues open to a blind person and so he learned to play the harp. Then, on horseback and with a helper, he travelled all over Connacht and Ulster, playing in the houses of better-off people and accepting their hospitality in return. He was a prolific composer, often writing pieces in honour of friends, generous patrons or beautiful women. He married a woman called Mary Maguire. The marriage was very happy and they had seven children. When she died Carolan wrote a beautiful poem in her honour containing the lines:

Fágadh 'na ndéidh sin liom féin mé go brónach
I ndeireadh mo shaoil 's gan mo chéile bheith beo agam.

[Bereft after that, alone and sorrowful
In my life's latter days, without the wife of my heart]

His last days were spent in travelling, playing the harp, composing and drinking more than was good for him. It is said he was not a great player as he came to the harp too late. But he was a good composer, influenced by the old harping tradition and also by the music of contemporaries like Vivaldi. His music was collected by people like Bunting* and it has remained popular down to the present day.

THE DUBLIN UNIONIST

Edward Carson (1854-1935)

Carson's life mirrors unionism in both its strengths and its weaknesses. Born into a bourgeois Dublin family on 9 February 1854 and given a good education at Trinity and King's Inns, he was a successful crown prosecutor first in an Ireland torn by land agitation and later in England where his most famous case was the prosecution of Oscar Wilde.* His appointment as solicitor-general to the government inevitably led him to into politics (MP for Dublin University) and attendance at Westminster inevitably to residence in London. He was twice a member of the British government (1900-6 and 1915-18). The union allowed an able Irishman to succeed in the wider world of British politics but Irish unionism was under threat from what its supporters saw as a narrowly nationalistic, Roman Catholic grouping, representative of the worst of Irish poverty and violence—the Irish party in Westminster. When an Irish nationalist majority persuaded a British liberal government to offer to give them Home Rule, Carson and the unionists joined with the British conservatives in organising armed resistance. In the unionist stronghold of Ulster arms were imported and the illegal Ulster Volunteers formed. At this point the war of 1914-18 broke out and Carson encouraged unionists to enlist in the army to prove their loyalty to Britain. After the War of Independence Britain agreed to independence for most of Ireland but kept the six most Protestant counties of Northern Ireland within the United Kingdom. For Carson it was only a partial victory and his last years in England were spent lamenting an Ireland that was gone and feeling no sympathy for the new nation that his fellow countrymen were struggling to build. He died in Kent on 22 October 1935 and is buried in St Anne's Cathedral in Belfast.

THE PROCONSULAR TRAITOR

Roger Casement (1864-1916)

Roger Casement was born in Dublin on 1 September 1864, the son of an army officer, but much of his early life was spent in Co Antrim where he attended Ballymena Academy. That county with its famous glens and especially Murlough Bay on the north coast near Fair Head was to be of great sentimental importance to him and he continually referred to Antrim in the diary he kept during the years he worked abroad. He went first to Africa as an officer of the colonial service and later was consul-general in Brazil. In both places he wrote reports which were highly critical of the treatment of native workers. He was knighted for his work in 1911 but he accepted the honour very unwillingly because already he was a committed Irish nationalist. He joined the Irish Volunteers in 1913, the year after he retired from the colonial service.

When Britain went to war against Germany in 1914 Casement travelled to Berlin and persuaded the High Command to give him arms to be used in the insurrection, planned for 1916. The shipment was intercepted and Casement was arrested at Banna Strand, Co Kerry. He was later hanged for high treason in Pentonville Gaol on 3 August 1916.

So ended the life of a great outsider; an Ulster Protestant who became a nationalist, a colonial civil servant who campaigned for native rights, and (worst of all for his reputation during his trial and after his death) a homosexual. In 1965 his remains were brought home for reinterment at Glasnevin (not his beloved Murlough). His homecoming inspired David Rudkin to write a play in which he sees Casement as:

"...a hero and not for Ireland only. For Ireland today, of course, he has an immediate, pressing relevance: with which of us, Ireland or England, must the Ulsterman Protestant in the end throw in his Red Hand? But Casement has a relevance to all mankind. He recreates himself in terms of his own inner truth. That act, courageous, at times humiliating and absurd, transcending poetry, lust and death, makes Roger Casement a hero for the world."

THE BIG FELLOW

Michael Collins (1890-1922)

The most famous photograph shows a big man in soldier's uniform with holster strapped to thigh—caught in a rare moment of stillness because Collins's short life was one of incessant activity. Born on a Co Cork farm, he emigrated to London to work in the post office. There he was won over to the IRB belief that force would win a worthwhile independence for Ireland. In the 1916 Rising Collins found himself a volunteer officer in the GPO, was later interned and kept until December 1916 in Frongoch prison camp in Wales. In the 1918 general election Collins and his Sinn Fein colleagues were given an overwhelming mandate by a public suddenly enthusiastic for a more advanced nationalism than that of the Irish party. When Sinn Fein decided to stay away from Westminster and formed the first Dáil in Dublin in 1919, Collins became Minister of Finance. He successfully organised a national loan and became the brilliant military brain behind the War of Independence, which also began in 1919. He maintained an intelligence system which prevented the British from getting to grips with the people who fought against them and goaded their troops into a fatal policy of reprisals and brutality against civilians, until finally this exhausting guerrilla war was brought to an end by a truce in 1921. At the end of that year a treaty was negotiated between Britain and Ireland which gave Ireland (minus the new state of Northern Ireland—the six counties of Ulster) "dominion status." Collins was one of the signatories and supported the treaty as a step on the way to full independence. The country, the IRA and the Dáil all split into pro-Treaty and anti-Treaty factions, although a majority supported the agreement. Collins made desperate attempts to prevent civil war, but was forced to take stern action against his opponents. Collins was killed soon after the outbreak of hostilities, when his convoy was ambushed while he was on an inspection tour as Commander-in-Chief of the Free State army. Béal na mBláth, where he was killed on 22 August 1922, was very near his birthplace and has since become a place of pilgrimage for those who admire Collins's charisma, effective leadership and ruthless pragmatism.

"PERIGRINATOR PRO CHRISTO"

St Colmcille (521-597)

1467 years ago a man was born of royal blood at Gartan in the heart of Donegal. He became a hero-figure with marvels and miracles attributed to him by later ages. It is hard to find the truth behind these wonderful stories but we know he did exist and that he founded monasteries in Swords, Durrow and Kells and, though there is no archaeological proof, in Derry, the town which in its Irish form, *Doire Cholmcille*, still bears his name. He was educated by St Finian at Clonard and was famous above all else for engaging in the work of inscribing the gospels in illuminated texts. and for supervising the work of others in the same field. One of the most famous stories tells of how he copied the psalter of St Finnian of Moville (not his old teacher) and had his copy, the work of many months, confiscated on the ruling of the Ard Rí Diarmaid, "to every cow its calf." This led to a struggle with the king which climaxed in the great battle of Cuildremhne near Sligo in 561 at which 3000 people were slain. His confessor, St Molaise, is said to have sent him to Scotland to win as many souls for Christ as were lost in the battle. He certainly sailed to Scotland with an apostolic twelve companions from Derry in 563 and founded the abbey of Iona where the marvellous Book of Kells was made. His biographer St Adamnan says merely that he went to Alba as "*perigrinator pro Christo*" [a pilgrim for Christ]. He is recorded as having only once returned to Ireland, as adviser to the great council of Drum Ceatt in 575. He died on 9 June 597. As well as being the hero of many stories he is also credited with much verse. His Latin verse, "*Altus Prosator*" shows him to have been a true poet. The *Cathach*, a Latin manuscript of the Psalms and the oldest surviving text in Ireland, is said to be in his handwriting.

THE LABOUR MEN

James Connolly (1868-1916) and James Larkin (1876-1947)

In early twentieth-century Ireland many people thought the struggle for better conditions for workers more important than the struggle for independence. Terrible urban poverty, especially in Dublin, cried out for redress. Two remarkable men, both born in Britain of emigrant parents, were to lead this labour movement. They were James Connolly, born in Edinburgh on 5 June 1868, and James Larkin, born in Liverpool on 21 January 1876.

Of the two, Connolly was the intellectual who gave

much of his time to applying Karl Marx's theories to Ireland's situation. In a series of books, *Labour in Irish History* being the best known, he tried to show that early Ireland had been an exemplary society and that a modern independent socialist Ireland would be similarly so. He founded the Irish Socialist Republican Party (ISRP) in 1896 and during a seven-year stay in America from 1903 to 1910 he was an organiser for the group known as the Industrial Workers of the World.

While Connolly was away trade unionism at home was to be galvanised by the boundless energy of Jim Larkin. He came first to Belfast where he organised a dock strike which was not completely successful because of religious divisions in the Belfast labour movement. He was the founder of the Irish Transport and General Workers Union, and led the Dublin workers during the famous lock-out of 1913, when employees who joined the ITGWU were refused work by the employers. The lock-out was only too successful and Larkin was imprisoned. After his release he went to the USA.

This left Connolly, who had returned to Ireland in 1910, as leader of the labour movement at a critical time in its history. The biggest union had been badly defeated in 1913. International socialism, in which Connolly fervently believed, had seemingly collapsed with the outbreak of a European war of nations in 1914. At home extreme nationalists prepared an insurrection, which Connolly with his Irish Citizen Army decided to join. He showed considerable military skill during the Rising and after the surrender was executed as one of the leaders on 12 May 1916. Connolly's more intellectual critics have been less than understanding of his decision to give his life for "a conspiracy of petit-bourgeois cultural nationalists."

Larkin's final part in the story was to become involved in the newly independent (though partitioned) Ireland which emerged after 1921. It was not to be the socialist paradise Connolly had fought and died for. Larkin as a Dáil deputy found himself at odds even with the Labour party because of his socialism. This same socialism was to see him expelled from the ITGWU and forced to form his own Workers Union of Ireland (WUI). To the end of his days Larkin continued his fight both in parliament and in the trade union movement for the cause of labour. Older Dublin people still remember fondly the sight of Larkin at public meetings with his arms outstretched and his wonderfully powerful voice.

THE FIRST ULSTER PREMIER

James Craig (1871-1940)

Protestant Ulster's victory (which resulted in the partition of Ireland in 1923) was to show that its people could dissent from the decision of the majority of their fellow Irishmen to become independent of Britain. This achievement was made possible by a mixture of charismatic leadership (by Carson) and efficient organisation. The latter was the work of James Craig, born on 8 January 1871, the son of a wealthy Belfast distiller, who, having organised and armed the illegal Ulster Volunteer Force (UVF) in 1912-14, served as quartermaster-general to the Ulster Division in the 1914-18 war. By the end of the war the six most Protestant counties of northern Ireland had won their struggle to remain within the United Kingdom, and the popular Craig was chosen as premier. He was not very successful in handling the inevitable problems of a statelet born of revolution. The failure of the relationship with the rest of Ireland was not entirely his fault, nor was the failure of an economy buffeted by a world depression. But his greatest mistake was that he made no attempt to woo the Catholic one-third of the population who saw the partition from the rest of the country as a disaster. He was created Viscount Craigavon of Stormont in 1927. As he got older he made less and less attempt to moderate the strongly anti-Catholic feeling of his supporters. The decline in his abilities was even more in evidence when he and his government were surprised by and totally unprepared for the coming of war in 1939. After his death on 24 November 1940 he was to be remembered by his followers as the first of those who saw themselves as Ulstermen rather than Irishmen.

THE CITIZEN

Michael Cusack (1847-1906)

During the rise of nationalism in the nineteenth-century many small subject countries including Czechoslovakia and Ireland used sports organisations as a way of expressing national difference and aspirations. One such organisation was the Gaelic Athletic Association (GAA), founded at a meeting in Hayes's Hotel, Thurles on 1 November 1884. The meeting had been called by Michael Cusack, a teacher born in Carron, Co Clare in 1847, who owned a cramming-school in Dublin. The success of his Civil Service Academy hurling club fired him to organise hurling (and football and athletics) countrywide in the new GAA. The association's national importance was marked by the fact that its patrons included a political leader, Parnell,* a sworn republican, Michael Davitt, and an archbishop, Thomas William Croke. The patrons, particularly Croke, did not find Cusack an easy man to work with and so within eighteen months of the founding of the association he was forced to resign his official connection with it. However, he lived to see his GAA winning over rural Ireland in a way that the romantic urban Gaelic League never could. And "The Citizen," as he liked to be addressed, was to be immortalised by a stand in Croke Park and described mockingly by James Joyce in *Ulysses* as "the barekneed brawnyhanded hairylegged ruddyfaced sinewyarmed hero...seated on a large boulder at the foot of a round tower."

THE MAN WHO BROUGHT THE TRAIN TO IRELAND

William Dargan (1799-1867)

Outside the National Gallery in Merrion Square stands the statue of a man. On the plinth is carved the one word *Dargan* and his gravestone in Glasnevin has the same stark simplicity. He was in his time a very rich man and as modest as his memorial stones suggest. (When Queen Victoria came to Ireland to see the Dublin Exhibition of 1853 she visited him in his own house in Dundrum and was not at all amused when he refused to accept the baronetcy she graciously offered.) He supplied the money for the building of the National Gallery but did not attend the ceremonial opening. Yet his patronage of art was not the main business of his life, for his money came from transport.

Dargan was born in Carlow on 28 February 1799 and studied engineering in England under Thomas Telford, the famous Scots bridge and road builder. His first Irish railroad ran from Westland Row station to what was then called Kingstown (now Dún Laoghaire). The first train ran on 17 December 1838, the locomotive with a tall smoke-stack like the one on George Stephenson's *Rocket* and the carriages looking like a line of stage-coaches strung together. He next built a canal to link Lough Erne and Lough Neagh and created out of the Lagan sandbanks the famous "Island" in Belfast Lough where the shipyard was later sited. His railways stretched north from Dublin to Drogheda, on both sides of Belfast Lough to Bangor and Carrickfergus and in time south and west to Cork. He loved modern science and all kinds of engineering schemes and when Prince Albert created the Great Exhibition in Hyde Park in 1851 he decided to do the same for Dublin. It was an exhibition of Art and Science and the pictures he acquired for it formed the nucleus of the gallery collection. The scheme netted him a loss of £20,000, a very large sum in today's money, but he thought it money well spent. He simply loved enterprises of that kind. He ran everything himself, so interested was he in all aspects of his work. The result was that when he was injured in a fall from a horse his business got into difficulties. He died on 2 February 1867, a month before his sixty-eighth birthday. His death was accelerated by what proved to be unnecessary worries about the business.

THE YOUNG IRELANDER

Thomas Davis (1814-45)

One night in 1840, a mature and notably serious final-year law student was giving his address as auditor to the Historical Association of Trinity College. He had been born in Mallow, Co Cork, on 14 October 1814 but he lived in Dublin for most of his life. The audience at auditor's nights never knew quite what to expect but on this occasion they were startled to hear an impassioned discourse on a country, the principle of whose separate existence they did not take seriously. "Gentlemen, you have a country...I do not fear that any of you will be found among Ireland's foes...Your country will, I fear, need all your devotion...She has no foreign friends...Beyond the limit of green Erin there is none to aid her." It was heady stuff, but Thomas Davis already knew that his purpose in life was to make Ireland, the land bled white, a nation once again. One of those listening to him that night was John Blake Dillon, a man who felt as Davis did, and he introduced him to a young Cavan journalist, John Gavan Duffy. Together they planned a new periodical, *The Nation,* the first number of which appeared on 15 October 1842. Its purpose was to teach nationhood to a depressed people. Davis wrote a great deal of the periodical's material on a wide variety of subjects. His style was severe but effective and his topics ranged from round towers to Ireland's economic resources. He was especially strong on the preservation of Irish as a spoken language: "To lose your native tongue and learn that of an alien is the worst badge of conquest—it is a chain on the soul." He was tired, too, of the national attitude of despondency and tried to raise the spirits of the nation with stirring ballads that recalled Ireland's former glories, such as "The West's Awake", "Clare's Dragoons", "Fontenoy" and his most famous poem, "A Nation Once Again." With *The Nation* he and his friends started the process which led to Ireland's moral and national recovery. He did not live to see much of the effect of his work because he died unexpectedly of scarlet fever on 16 September 1845 and was buried in Mount Jerome cemetery in Dublin. The Young Ireland that he had helped to create had to face the terrible famine of the mid-1840s and many other later setbacks but the seeds of nationhood which he set were well tended and they survived triumphantly.

THE IRISH STATESMAN

Eamon de Valera (1882-1975)

To the plain people of Clare who continued to choose him
as their Dáil deputy for over thirty-five years he was "the
long fellow," a tall thin bespectacled man in a long dark coat
who addressed them in a flat Limerick accent. He had a
charisma, a magic which silenced even the hecklers of the
opposition Fine Gael. He promoted an ideal, an Ireland
where freedom and frugal comfort would make people
happy.

For historians he is a master politician who talked of
ideals but always acted pragmatically. The commander at

Boland's Mills in the 1916 uprising, he was sentenced to death but this sentence was later commuted to one of life-imprisonment. Released in 1917, he won the Clare by-election. Dev, as he became universally known, was made president of Sinn Féin and so president of the revolutionary Dáil Éireann called by Sinn Féin after their landslide victory in the 1918 election. In 1922 he led a minority out of the Dáil, protesting that the Treaty did not allow full independence from Britain. Yet five years later he had formed a new party, Fianna Fáil, got the support of those who had opposed the government in the civil war and so won over a group who believed in using force to a belief in politics. In two other major sectors Dev followed the same strategy of mixing the ideal and the practical. Between 1932 and 1945 he broke, one by one, the remaining constitutional links with Britain but always realised the importance of the British market for Ireland. For example, as soon as the "economic war" had achieved its political purpose he very quickly moved again to a position of trade reciprocity with Britain. And although he claimed a 32-county Ireland (in the constitution of 1937), he realised that Northern unionists could not be coerced out of the United Kingdom.

To the world he was the only Irish statesman. He had been a major figure in the work for peace of the League of Nations in the 1930s. When that work failed and war broke out, he had, against all odds, kept his country neutral. Later, as president, he was there to welcome both De Gaulle and John F Kennedy to Ireland. When he died in 1975, a few months after his wife Sinéad, he was almost the last of those whose political careers began with the 1916 rising.

EMMET'S COURIER

Anne Devlin (c. 1778-1851)

Anne Devlin was the daughter of Big Arthur Devlin and so a cousin of Michael Dwyer, the 1798 rebel from Wicklow. Both her father and cousin were part of Robert Emmet*'s plans for another uprising in 1803. Emmet needed a trustworthy servant to help him communicate with his lieutenants and the daughter of a father committed to the rising seemed the ideal person.

So Anne found herself living in the house at Rathfarnham where Emmet, using the name of Ellis, had his quarters. From there she took messages into the old city where plans were being laid and weapons made for the insurrection. She also carried letters to Sarah, the daughter of John Philpot Curran, with whom Emmet had fallen in love. On the morning of the uprising Anne delivered clean linen so that the leader should look well; that night she met the leaders in flight from the failure and led them to the safety of her father's house. When Emmet left the refuge of the mountains to see his beloved Sarah, he was arrested and brought to trial. In the search for evidence against Emmet, the Devlins were arrested. Anne refused the offer of a bribe from Major Sirr, who was interrogating her, with such well-chosen oaths that they made even the hardened soldier blanch. She successfully hid her shock at being suddenly confronted with Emmet. "Not for the whole world would I swear one syllable against you," she whispered to him. Questioned again on the day of Emmet's execution, and taken to see the gallows the day after, she refused to speak. She was not released from Kilmainham till 1806. In poverty she lived on in Dublin, forgotten by all save Dr Madden whom she helped with his history of the United Irishmen. From 1851, when Madden put a stone over her grave, to 1987, when Pat Murphy made her the subject of a feminist film epic, her fame has grown and grown.

"WEE JOE"

Joseph Devlin (1879-1934)

On any good summer's day during the first thirty years of
this century, among the crowds of poor Belfast children
who were taken on outings to the seaside at Portrush or
Bangor, you might easily have seen a small man with a big
head playing on the sands as happily as any child. He was
the one who paid for the excursions and he had also found
the money to set up a holiday home for Belfast female
workers who could not afford a vacation. He came from
working-class Belfast and was loved and respected even by
his political opponents. He was "Wee Joe" to everybody.

71

The son of a jarvey, Joseph Devlin was born on 13 February 1879, in Hamill Street at the bottom of the Falls Road. He became a journalist with the *Irish News* in 1891 and was by this time a formidable debater. In 1902 he was returned unopposed as Irish Party MP for N Kilkenny and in 1906 he recovered the West Belfast seat which had been lost to a unionist in 1892. He held this seat until 1918. He re-established the moribund Ancient Order of Hibernians and remained president till his death. He was offered the leadership of the Irish party on the death of John Redmond but relinquished it to John Dillon. The success of Sinn Féin in the 1918 election meant the end of his party though he had a personal victory over de Valera* in the Falls constituency. He also became an MP for the new Stormont parliament though he rarely attended the sessions. His only course of action that might have led to violence was his organisation of National Volunteers to counter Carson*'s Ulster Volunteers. After 1923 he was content to be a constituency politician, accessible to his people, and he avoided wider involvement. He served the Belfast Catholics until his death in 18 January 1934. His funeral was the largest ever seen in his native city.

THE LEGIONARY

Frank Duff (1889-1980)

"Religion has become a routine. A terrible conservatism exercises relentless sway...Even when the world has more or less taken up the Legion, Ireland looks at it suspiciously." By the 1940s the Legion of Mary which the Dublin-born civil servant, Frank Duff, had founded in 1921 had spread as far afield as Australia and China. Duff himself had been received and commended by Pius XI. Yet at home the archbishop of Dublin was so suspicious of lay action that he did not give the *Legio Mariae* handbook his *imprimatur* till 1953, the Jesuits feared competition from Duff's movement and the intellectuals were cynical of Duff's "miraculous meddlers." Duff remained undaunted by opposition, inspired by Louis-Marie de Montfort's idea of "true devotion" to the Virgin Mary and by a belief in lay evangelism. With his fellow legionaries he worked for the care of the homeless at the Morning Star hostel and for the reform of prostitutes in the nearby Sancta Maria hostel. Later he worked as a full-time director of the Legion at de Montfort house. He attended Vatican II as a lay observer, but he was critical of what he considered "false ecumenism," and of a changing view of the Virgin Mary. He continued to work for his beloved Legion until he died on 7 November 1980. Up to a very short time before his death he was still making his way round Dublin, as he had always done, on a bicycle.

THE MOSTRIM NOVELIST

Maria Edgeworth (1767-1849)

If you are the dutiful eldest daughter of a loved father who married four times, the chances are that you will spend a lot of your time looking after step-sisters and -brothers. Such was indeed the fate of Maria Edgeworth who helped to educate her eighteen siblings at the family mansion in Edgeworthstown, Co Longford. She was born on 1 January 1767, the daughter of a man who believed like Rousseau that children should be allowed to develop naturally. Together they wrote of their system in *Practical Education* (1798). Part of the child's education entailed the reading of moral tales and Maria showed great skill in writing these. She then went on to write a number of novels, one of which, *Castle Rackrent*, has ensured her a place not just in Irish but also in the literary history of the English-speaking world. In a brief text the old servant Thady M'Quirk tells the story of the decline of the Rackrent family over four generations, "Sir Patrick by drink, Sir Murtagh by law, Sir Kit by gambling, and Sir Condy...by politics." The book is a very funny account of the relationship between the Catholic tenants and their Protestant landlord masters but like all great writing it has more than one facet. It is also a requiem for the death of an era when landlord control was unquestioned, and a warning that if the Anglo-Irish aristocracy wish to retain influence they must act responsibly (a theme to which she returns in *The Absentee* (1812) and in *Ormond* (1817). When her father died she was left to run the family estate in an Ireland for which she felt more and more fearful. She barely outlived (22 May 1849) the disastrous famine which swept away so many of her countrymen in the 1840s. She was remembered by her surviving tenants with gratitude for all she had done for them during their trials, and by the literary world for her influence on Walter Scott, and through him on the nineteenth-century French and Russian realists.

THE DARLING OF ERIN

Robert Emmet (1778-1803)

"Bold Robert Emmet" is remembered as the man who, dressed in green coat, white breeches and cocked hat, led his small band of followers on foot to attack Dublin Castle. The castle guard had got word of the attack at the last minute and they closed the gates. Emmet fled to the Dublin mountains but then returned to a hiding-place at Harold's Cross where he was able to see his beloved Sarah Curran. While in her company he was captured, and after a trial and a famous speech ("When my country takes her place among the nations of the earth, then and not till then, let my epitaph be written") he was hanged at Thomas Street.

Emmet's love affair with Sarah inspired Thomas Moore to write one of his loveliest songs, "She Is Far From the Land." The image of a brave man attempting a revolution against the might of England with one hundred followers was to be a potent one for Pearse* and the men of 1916.

It now seems that the picture of a "brave but foolish man" was put about by the government of the time to hide the fact that they had been caught totally unawares by Emmet's planned insurrection. They do not seem to have known that he and his brother Thomas were in Paris canvassing Napoleon and Talleyrand for help with an uprising. The network of old United Irishmen in Wicklow and Down had no idea of the weaponry amassed at various locations in Dublin city. But for an accidental explosion at a rebel depot in Patrick Street, the government would have had no inkling of what was happening and Emmett's uprising might have been a much greater test of its ability to control Ireland. Not that this would have made Emmet any more famous than he has become. Where popular fame in the matter of insurrections is concerned, nothing succeeds like failure.

THE MAN ON THE FIVE-POUND NOTE

Johannes Scotus Eriugena (c.810-877)

You have all seen the tough-looking man on the Irish five-pound note. In his time he was the greatest Greek scholar in Western Europe and he was the greatest Irish philosopher before George Berkeley. As the second and third words of his name make clear he was Irish-born. After a monastic education he went to the court of Charles the Bald in France and there translated many theological works into Latin, the common language of the civilised world.

His greatest work and one which got him into trouble with the Pope was *Peri Phuseon*, known in Latin as *De*

Divisione Naturae and completed by him in 866. It was meant to define the structure of the universe. Man is a certain intellectual idea formed eternally in the mind of God. God is essentially good and could not create Hell as a place of punishment. Hell is a state of mind which the sinful bring about in themselves. The implication that evil could not exist caused the book to be listed in the *Index of Prohibited Books*. It is only now in the 20th Century that it has gained any orthodoxy. Two legends have attached themselves to Eriugena. One is that once while at table with King Charles he was regally asked what was the difference between an Irishman and a drunkard (*Scotus* and *sottus*). To this he answered, "The width of a table." The other is that when Charles died in 877, Eriugena went to teach in England and was killed by angry students; perhaps, as someone said, it was because he tried to make them think.

THE TRACTOR MAN

Harry Ferguson (1884-1960)

On 31 December 1908, a young Irish inventor climbed into a monoplane that he had built and flew in it for the greatest distance that any heavier-than-air machine had achieved up to that, 130 yards. It was only four years since the Wright brothers' first ever flight at Kitty Hawk and here was Ireland's first air journey in the grounds of Lord Downshire's estate at Hillsborough, Co Down on a day of fierce wind. The gallant aviator was Harry George Ferguson and he had been born not far away, at Growell, on 4 November 1884. By the age of sixteen "the mad mechanic," as he was called because of his reckless skill at motorcycle-racing, had set up his own garage in Belfast.

It was as an inventor that he became world famous. His development of the tractor and of the capability of linking to it many of his own implements including the moulded plough had made him a very rich man. In 1939 he demonstrated his tractor plough for Henry Ford, the automobile king, and they made a "handshake agreement" to produce the Fordson tractor, a title derived from their surnames. The design and continuing modifications were to be done by Ferguson and the marketing by Ford. In 1947 this unwritten contract was repudiated by Ford's son and after a four-year legal action, Ferguson was compensated with a four-million dollar settlement. He continued to work on chassis design and automatic transmission until his death in his Gloucestershire home at Stow-in-the-Wold on 25 October 1960. He had been offered a knighthood for his inventive services to the Allies during the Second World War but he refused it. His revolutionary ideas on traction are still regarded as worth developing.

THE MAN WHO WROTE NOCTURNES

John Field (1732-1837)

Until the recital room in the National Concert Hall was named in his honour John Field was certainly better known in Russia than in Ireland. Though he spent only eleven years in his native Dublin it was there he learnt his music from his father, a violinist at the Crow Street Theatre, and from Giordani, the composer-in-residence at the Smock Alley Theatre. At ten years of age he amazed his fellow Dubliners by playing a complete piano concerto by Giordani at the Rotunda Concert Rooms. It was soon after this that he moved to London, met Clementi and began to be known all over musical Europe.

After a tour of London, Paris and Vienna he came to Petrograd and settled there. He was the illustrious teacher of Glinka (who wrote the first Russian opera) a prolific composer of concertos and sonatas, but he was above all the originator of that short, slow piano piece in which a melody is accompanied by broken chords, the nocturne. He composed twenty of these though his are not as well known as those of Chopin who made the form much more romantic.

In later life Field was often ill through drinking too much but the Russians remained understanding of him and gave him a great public funeral to Moscow's Wedensky Cemetery. On his tombstone they proudly wrote that he had died in their beloved Moscow. They did not, however, forget to write that he had been born in Ireland. Great pianist, prolific composer, famous teacher, originator of the nocturne, John Field deserves to be better known in his native land.

THE AVIATOR

Col. James Fitzmaurice (1898-1965)

The years after the first world war which saw the
independent Irish state come into being were also to be the
heyday of the aeroplane. The new state's geographical
position, as the nearest part of Europe to America, ensured
that it would play a part in the story of aviation. The first
west-east transatlantic flight (that of Alcock and Whitten-
Brown) had landed in Co Galway, at the time when James
Fitzmaurice tried to raise money for an Irish attempt on the
more difficult westward crossing. Fitzmaurice was a
Dubliner, born on 6 January 1898, who had learned to fly

with the Royal Flying Corps during the war and then transferred to the new Irish Air Corps. There he found the routine of training airmen boring and when the attempt to organise a totally Irish flight failed, he joined the Germans Von Hünefeld and Köhl in the *Bremen* which took off from Baldonnell airfield on 12 April 1928. Nearly thirty-seven hours later they landed in Labrador, the first to make the westward journey. Fitzmaurice liked America, and after failing to interest the Irish government in a civilian air service, he returned there. He went to England in 1939 and stayed there for the war years, running a services club, but he came back to live in Dublin in 1951. He had a last moment of glory in 1953 when he was invited to Bremen to commemorate the twenty-fifth anniversary of the great transatlantic achievement. By then his native country had established an airport at Shannon for transatlantic flights and an airline which was to go from success to success. He died in Dublin in September 1965.

THE HEADLINE MAN

Vere Foster (1819-1900)

If you had gone into any primary school in Ireland between the years 1860 and 1945 you would have seen the pupils writing with pen and ink on copybooks (the ballpoint was not invented till 1943). The chances are that they would have been copying one of a number of "headlines" already printed in their books. These headlines were usually proverbs or moral precepts, such as: "Habits may gain a Samson's strength" or "The more haste, the less speed." The man responsible for these copybooks was Vere Foster, a rich man who spent two fortunes on the poor, and who had only

£178 in his possession when he died in Belfast on 21 December 1900. Foster was born on 26 April 1819 in Copenhagen where his Irish father was British Minister. He himself served in the diplomatic service in South America. In 1847 he heard of the potato famine in Ireland and, returning to the family estates in Co Louth, was so horrified by the misery he saw that he spent the rest of his life working for the good of the Irish poor. He soon realised that one way to relieve the recurring famines was to encourage voluntary emigration. He provided the passage money for many emigrants out of his own pocket and travelled on emigrant ships to see for himself just how bad conditions really were. He kept a journal of his experiences and his report was so damning that laws were passed in parliament that ended the harsh treatment of the travellers. He wrote pamphlets for intending emigrants and gave them good advice about how to survive in the New World. He understood that education was most important and he did everything he could to improve Irish schools. He built new schools himself and refurbished older ones. He designed and marketed the famous copybooks and organised teachers into a professional association which eventually became the Irish National Teachers Organisation. He was one of the really great Irishmen of his time.

THE SINGING ENGINEER

Percy French (1854-1920)

You've all heard, probably even sung, "Phil the Fluther's Ball" and joined in "The Mountains of Mourne" or "Slattery's Mounted Fut." They were all written (and first sung) by a man who started out in life as a civil engineer. Percy French was born in Clooneyquin, Co Roscommon, on 1 May 1854 and having eventually graduated from Trinity became Inspector of Drains for Co Cavan in 1881. When his first wife died and a career as a comic journalist failed, he became an entertainer, travelling the country and writing all his own material. His shows were very popular because he was a skilled banjoist, a clever reciter and a fine singer of his own songs. But the list of his talents doesn't stop there. He was an excellent artist who used to paint watercolours on stage and give them away to members of the audience. He could even draw pictures on plates with the smoke of a candle. He wrote songs and recitations about many different places, from "The Darling Girl from Clare" to "The Pride of Petravore." His first song "Abdul the Bulbul Ameer" was for many years believed to be an anonymous American student song. He wrote about golf, tennis and horse-racing and about the newly-invented means of transport: "Flanagan's Flying Machine", "Maguire's Motor Bike", "Jim Whelehan's Automobile." One of his most famous songs, "Are You Right There, Michael?" was about the West Clare Railway and this led to a libel action. He died in Formby, Lancashire, on 24 January 1920.

PADDY THE COPE

Patrick Gallagher (1873-1964)

There was once a song that began, "Paddy the Cope has a shop in Dungloe." Cope was the local version of the word "co-op" and the shop (now indeed several shops) still flourishes, the pride of the "capital of the Rosses." The man who began the Templecrone Cooperative Society and broke the power of local "gombeen" men was born on Christmas Day 1873, the eldest of nine children, on a farm of reclaimed bogland at Cleendra some miles from Dungloe. The area was so poor that ploughs were unknown and the land had to be prepared for tillage by spade. Like all the able-bodied children of the region he was hired out from the age of ten as a badly-paid farm-hand in the fertile Laggan district which comprises the basin of the Foyle river and its tributaries. He received £3 for his first six months work. Each of the next six hiring-seasons (usually from May till October) was spent in the Laggan and then he went as was the custom to earn somewhat better wages in much worse conditions in Scotland. He saved enough money in the Pumperstown Co-op to buy a farm at home (and to use on it the district's first plough.) He had also become an ardent advocate of co-operation and a follower of the ideas of AE and Sir Horace Plunkett.* The local traders supplied goods at high rates of interest and accepted in lieu of payment the knitting produced by the sweated labour of the Rosses womenfolk. Quite naturally these traders resisted the establishment of the co-op and began a campaign of character-assassination by suggesting that Paddy Pat Bán (as he was locally known) was financed by Protestants. But the people soon saw the advantages of buying in their own store and making profits for themselves. The society prospered. Paddy was able to bring in supplies by sea to Burtonport when the Rosses was blockaded by the Black and Tans. He built a pier at Dungloe which is at the head of a tidal bay and had a generator set up that supplied power free to the churches and lit the main street. He exported knitwear and flagstones and generally did everything he could to improve the amenities in the town. AE urged him to write his autobiography which he did in a best-selling book called simply *My Story* which was published in 1939. Paddy the Cope died on 24 June 1964.

THE GREAT EARL

Gerald (Garret Mór) Fitzgerald Earl of Kildare (died 1513)

In these islands the fifteenth century was a time of civil war; in England the Wars of the Roses were being fought out between the houses of York and Lancaster; in Ireland the Anglo-Irish earls fought the Gaelic chieftains and both sides fought among themselves. Those people who lived in the English part of Ireland—the Pale, the lands round Dublin and north to Meath—often felt as much at risk from the earls who had adopted Irish ways and paid only token loyalty to the English crown, as from the Gaels. Yet even the Irish-speaking earls could not help being influenced by English affairs and different families took different sides on the struggle in England. The Fitzgeralds supported the Yorkists and prospered while Edward IV and Richard III were on the throne, while the Butlers of Ormond were advanced during the long reign of Henry VI. Garret Mór, eighth Earl of Kildare, was the most powerful man in Ireland during England's turmoil but his position became doubtful when the first Tudor king, Henry VII, obtained the throne after defeating and killing Richard III at Bosworth Field. He supported a Yorkist pretender to the throne called Lambert Simnel who was crowned king in Dublin and later he was accused (though this was not proven) of favouring a much more serious contender called Perkin Warbeck. In spite of this Henry pardoned him and allowed him to act as the king's deputy for his lifetime. As Henry is reported to have said, "Since all Ireland cannot rule this man, this man must rule all Ireland." If Garret had been more of a statesman and less loyal to the king he could have made himself ruler of an independent Ireland and perhaps changed the course of Irish history. As it was, Henry VIII who succeeded his father in 1509 proved a stronger and less tolerant ruler. He imprisoned Garret Óg, Kildare's son, and beheaded his grandson, "Silken" Thomas. The Great Earl was shot dead by a musket-ball in a battle with O'Carroll of Offaly.

POOR POLL

Oliver Goldsmith (1728-74)

One night in the middle of the eighteenth century a young
Trinity man was on a journey from Dublin to his home in
Lissoy, Co Westmeath. He reached the village of Ardagh,
Co Longford, and realised he would have to spend the night
there. He asked the advice of drinking companions in the
local ale-house about a suitable inn and they directed him
to "the best house in the village." The young man caused
much anger to the people who owned the house and much
embarrassment to himself by treating the place as an inn but
the incident provided the germ of the plot of the man's most

famous play, *She Stoops to Conquer*. It was typical of the life of Oliver Goldsmith, son of the rector of Lissoy. Born on 10 November 1728 in Pallas, Co Longford, where his father, Charles Goldsmith, was curate, he had a career full of such misadventures. He had an undistinguished record at Trinity and later spent several years at the universities of Edinburgh and Leyden (in Holland). He returned to London claiming to have a medical degree. He is said to have kept himself alive on his wanderings by playing the flute.

In London he became a denizen of Grub Street—a general term for those who lived by writing poems, articles and even books to order. He was unusual among the other hacks in that he was a genius and anything he wrote was distinguished. *The Citizen of the World* (1762) is one of the finest books of essays in English just as *She Stoops to Conquer* (1773) is one of the finest stage comedies, *The Deserted Village* (1770) one of the best long poems and *The Vicar of Wakefield* (1766) a great short novel.

Goldsmith was always short of money, partly because of his addiction to gambling and partly because of his generosity to the poor, whom he treated free of charge. He was a member of Dr Johnson's famous "Club" but he never shone as a talker. As David Garrick once said in a mock epitaph:

> *Here lies Nolly Goldsmith, for shortness called Noll,*
> *Who wrote like an angel but talked like poor Poll.*

He died of fever, aggravated by worry about debts, on 4 April 1774.

A MOST FAMOUS FEMININE SEA-CAPTAIN

Gráinne Ní Mháille (c.1530-1600)

Clew Bay in Co Mayo is full of islands and the largest, Clare Island, guards the entrance of the bay. From this island for much of the sixteenth-century a famous sea-rover ruled the waters of western Ireland. She was Granuaile [Grace of Umhall] and she regarded herself as a queen. Certainly when she visited the court of Elizabeth I of England she spoke as queen to queen. She died in poverty on Clare Island and is buried there. It does not take much imagination to picture her there, an old woman of seventy, dreaming of her exciting life. She married twice, first Donal

97

O'Flaherty, lord of Ballynahinch, and when he died, Richard (of the Iron) Burke. Using fast-moving galleys she attacked many ships which sailed near her territory. Once she successfully beat off the assault of an English fleet on her husband's stronghold at Carrighooly, near Newport. Her son *Tiobóid na Long* [Theobald of the Ships] was made first Viscount of Mayo but Grace's loyalty to England could not be guaranteed. One of her enemies, Sir Henry Sidney, called her "a most famous feminine sea-captain" and Sir Richard Bingham, Elizabeth's viceroy in Mayo, harassed her for most of her life. Once she had to take refuge with O'Neill* in Ulster. She died in 1600 before the Gaelic world she knew received its death-blow at Kinsale.

THE PARLIAMENTARIAN

Henry Grattan (1746-1820)

Across the road from Trinity College, the House of Commons was in session. In the Parliament building there was a hush as Henry Grattan, the MP for Charlemont, stood to speak. The young Dublin-born (3 July 1746) Trinity-educated barrister was already by 1780 a well-known voice in the chamber. He did not disappoint his listeners. They cheered his, "never was there a parliament in Ireland so possessed of the confidence of the people…", became more enthusiastic as he warmed to his subject and erupted when he finished with the immortal words "…a country as enlightened as Ireland, chartered as Ireland, armed as Ireland, and injured as Ireland, will be satisfied with nothing less than liberty." Soon afterwards the British government gave the Irish parliament sole right to make laws for Ireland. Grattan and his Patriot party had won a great victory.

The Irish "patriots" were following the example of the American colonists who had just declared their independence from Britain. Like the Americans, the members of the Irish parliament were descended from settlers who had come from Britain more than two centuries earlier, and like the Americans they felt they could rule themselves. But unlike the Americans, who could treat the Indian natives as savages with no rights, the Patriots who were Protestants were unsure how to treat the native Irish Catholics. Most believed they should remain without any power in the new independent parliament. A minority led by Grattan believed that Catholics must be given political rights. Grattan continued to support Catholic relief in Parliament but his gradualism proved unsatisfactory to the radical United Irishmen. The 1798 rising led inevitably to the Act of Union with Britain. Grattan continued to speak for the Catholics in the united parliament at Westminster. On his way there in May 1820, too ill to travel by coach over bumpy roads and yet determined to speak in the House of Commons, he made the journey from Liverpool by canal barge. He died in London on 4 June of that year and was buried in Westminster Abbey.

DESIGNING WOMAN

Eileen Gray (1887-1976)

The upper struts of the frame are horizontal and the rear ones vertical but the lower and forward bars are at such angles as to make the shape irregularly quadrilateral. The frame is of black lacquer held together with brass fittings. The brown leather cover falls in a graceful curve from the rear of the frame and then rises a little to join a crossbar in front. With its clean bare lines it is a classic armchair design of the 1920s. Its designer lived on the rue Bonaparte and owned the Galerie Jean Désert at 271 rue du Faubourg St-Honoré. She was born Eileen Gray at Brownswood House near Enniscorthy in 1887. She trained as an artist in London and Paris. In the latter city the Japanese Sugawara taught her how to work with lacquer. Her career was interrupted by the First World War during which she drove an ambulance. She went on to become one of the most admired furniture designers of her day. Later she became interested in architecture and had houses built to her own design at Roquebrune and Castellar on the Côte d'Azur. The house at Roquebrune was considered a masterpiece of modern architecture by no less an expert than Le Corbusier. As late as 1945 she revisited the country of her birth but it was not until 1973 that her country offered her the accolade of an honorary fellowship of the Royal Institute of Architects of Ireland. Her other great love was of aviation and she took part in several early flights. She died in the same apartment in the rue Bonaparte to which she had come to live in 1907 and was buried at Père Lachaise cemetery.

THE PLAYWRIGHT WITH THE CAKE

Augusta, Lady Gregory (1852-1932)

The early days of the Abbey Theatre were often financially unstable. At times there was not enough money to pay the actors and rehearsals got a bit gloomy. Then a small lady, dressed all in black, as widows usually were in those days, would arrive off the Galway train with a huge cake and the tea-party that followed would cheer everybody up. This was typical of the quiet, practical way in which she helped the young theatre to survive. She was born Augusta Persse on 15 March 1852 at Roxborough House, Co Galway. Though Anglo-Irish she was strongly influenced by her

Irish-speaking nurse Mary Sheridan. She married Sir William Gregory of Coole Park, Gort, in 1880 and when he died in 1892 she renewed her interest in Irish culture. She became a friend of Douglas Hyde* and W B Yeats* and published *Cuchulain of Muirthemne*, a fine retelling of the old Irish sagas, in 1902. She followed this in 1904 by more Celtic tales, *Gods and Fighting Men*.

The idea of a national theatre came about because of a conversation on a wet afternoon between Lady Gregory, Edward Martyn, a Catholic Galway landowner, and Yeats. The Abbey Theatre movement started with a public statement from the three founders which began with the words, "We propose to have performed in Dublin, in the spring of every year, certain Celtic and Irish plays..." Lady Gregory wrote twenty-seven plays for their theatre, most composed in a kind of English that seemed to be translated literally from the Irish and which was dubbed Kiltartan from the name of a village on the Gregory estate at Coole. The most famous of these, *Spreading the News*, *The Gaol Gate* and *The Rising of The Moon*, are often revived. She acted as a calming influence on her more extreme partners and often smoothed awkward situations with her commonsense approach. She died on 22 May 1932 at Coole. Her only son, Major Robert Gregory, was killed in France during the First World War.

THE FIRST SINN FÉINER

Arthur Griffith (1871-1922)

Arthur Griffith was the populariser of an inspired political slogan, Sinn Féin (which is still used today) and of an original policy for winning Irish independence which was perhaps inevitably perverted. He was born in Dublin on 31 March 1871 and earned his living as a printer and journalist. He lived in South Africa for the two years 1896-98 working in the goldmines and there he became impressed by Boer resistance to British rule. He was also impressed by what he had read of Hungary's struggle to be free of Austria and wrote a book *The Resurrection of Hungary* in 1904. He maintained that the same tactics could be used in Ireland: the simple withdrawal of support from British institutions. He launched Sinn Féin to spread these ideas but a large early membership fell away as the years went by and nothing happened. Then all was changed with the advent of the European war of 1914, a war which encouraged the more advanced nationalists to rise in 1916. The British suppressed this rising with impolitic severity. Released from prison under amnesty the new heroes of the rising seized on the title Sinn Féin for their new political organisation. They followed Griffith's policy of withdrawing from Westminster and meeting together in Dublin as the first Dáil in 1919. Griffith became one of the leaders but could not prevent force being used to defend the new institutions, first against the British, and then, after independence, against those who rejected the treaty. Arthur Griffith was one of the signatories and was president of the new Irish Free State when he died of cerebral haemorrhage on 28 June 1922. He left a wife and two children and the masterfully simple slogan, Sinn Féin, which was to be used by a kaleidoscopic range of groupings believing almost always that something was wrong with the country and that force was the only way to cure things.

THE PROTESTANT BREWER

Arthur Guinness (1725-1803)

In 1798, to show his disapproval of the United Irishmen's rebellion, the Dublin brewer whose name has persisted to this day began to market "Guinness's black Protestant porter." The great Irish drink had arrived. Arthur Guinness, the determinedly sectarian brewer, was born in Celbridge in 1725 and began his career as an ale-maker in Leixlip. He moved to the city in 1759 and bought the brewery which is still sited at St James's Gate. The name of his black porter did not please Dublin Catholic drinkers so they boycotted it and the brewery but Arthur, tirelessly enterprising, used the time of the boycott to begin a very profitable export trade to England. This stand was typical of the fiery brewer who had in 1775 defied the city council's officers over water supply and was prepared to defend what he saw as his rights by personal violence if necessary. That matter was settled peacefully and in time the whole urban population was reconciled to his drink. Succeeding generations of the family became benefactors of the city. The founding father became master of the Dublin Corporation of Brewers with a seat on the city council. He founded the first Sunday school in Ireland in 1786 and died in 1803.

THE GENIUS GRAFFITIST

Sir William Rowan Hamilton (1805 -1865)

One autumn day in the year 1843 a thirty-eight year old man was walking with his wife by the Royal canal in Dublin. He had not said very much (he was often lost in thought) but all of a sudden he whipped out his penknife and carved something on the parapet of Broom bridge. It would have been very odd behaviour for any man of his age but for the Irish Astronomer Royal it was unthinkable; except that, well, he was a genius.

Rowan Hamilton was born at 36 Dominick Street, Dublin, on 4 August 1805. By the age of seven he knew nine languages, including Hebrew, Latin and Greek, and by the time he was twelve he had added Persian, Arabic, Sanskrit, Hindustani and Malay. He started his study of mathematics by reading Euclid in the original Greek. Small wonder he was made professor of astronomy at Trinity and Astronomer Royal at the age of twenty-two, and knighted at thirty for services to science. Yet his strongest personal ambition was to be a poet and he was a close friend of William Wordsworth and Robert Southey. He was, however, justly proud of Ireland's position in the world of science and declared that she had replaced France as mathematics leader of the world. He died on 2 September 1865 having had many honours thrust upon him. What he wrote on the bridge was: $i^2 = j^2 = k^2 = ijk = -1$, the basis of his theory of quaternions which paved the way for quantum mechanics and nuclear physics. If you can understand this then you are a budding Rowan Hamilton yourself for i, j and k represent $\sqrt{-1}$ in the three different dimensions of the Cartesian plane.

THE FENIAN RAMMER

John Philip Holland (1841-1914)

The craft was 17m long and displaced 75 tonnes, an electric motor gave her a speed of 6 knots and she had a cruising range of 2400 km. For weaponry she used both torpedoes and dynamite shells. She could dive to 9m in 5 seconds and could travel 80km underwater. She greatly impressed the US Navy Board who had done a study of her and so she became the first of her kind to be commissioned into any navy. She was the first submarine, the USS *Holland* and she was called after her inventor, John Philip Holland, who was born in Liscannor, Co Clare on 24 February 1841.

He was the son of a coastguard and would have become a seaman but that his eyesight was poor. Instead he became an Irish Christian Brother and taught in schools in different parts of the country for fourteen years. In 1872 he went to America, having left the congregation, and began to look for backing for his idea of an undersea boat. John Devoy, the Fenian leader, thought that such an invention could be used to attack the British navy and so provided Holland with enough money to build the "Fenian Ram." This was Holland's first successful craft and this prototype led directly to the modified design which was accepted by the US Navy.

Holland was more successful as an inventor than as a businessman, and though his ideas were taken up by the British, Russian and Japanese navies, he never became rich and died just before his invention proved its deadly usefulness in the world war of 1914-18. He died in Newark, NJ on 12 August 1914.

THE EXILE WHO NEVER LEFT DUBLIN

James Joyce (1882-1941)

"Once upon a time and a very good time it was there was a moocow coming down along the road…" The opening words of *A Portrait of the Artist as a Young Man* show this son of a bourgeois Dublin family, born on Candlemas Day, 1882, to be already a writer. Using a style suitable to each theme he describes his childhood, his education at Clongowes and at Belvedere, his father's inability to support the family, his religious elation followed by loss of faith, his resolve to become a great artist, his time at UCD, and finally his decision to leave Ireland.

With him to Zürich, then Trieste and finally Paris, went his beloved, Nora Barnacle. An exile, he set his next book in his native Dublin on the day on which he left, 16 June 1904. In a wonderful variety of styles he tells of the doings of Leopold Bloom, Stephen Dedalus and other citizens on that one day. Published in Paris in 1922, *Ulysses* is a landmark in the history of modern literature.

In his later years Joyce gradually went blind but with the help of friends he produced his final great work *Finnegans Wake*. Once again the exile wrote of his long-abandoned city but this time in the form of a dream and using not just a variety of styles but also of languages. Before leaving Paris for Zürich where he died on 13 January 1941, he wrote the book's last words: "Finn, again! Take. Bussoftlhee, mememormee! Till thousendsthee. Lps. The keys to. Given! A way a lone a last a loved a long the."

LORD HAW-HAW

William Joyce (1906-1946)

"Once again steel meets steel and I can tell you that here in Germany there is perfect and wholehearted confidence in the certainty of victory. In Britain of late the opinion is often being expressed that 1943 will prove a year of decision. On this proposition I give no judgement for the moment, but of one thing I am sure, 1943 will be a year of most unpleasant surprises for Germany's enemies.

Germany calling. You have just been listening to 'Views on the News' by William Joyce. Thank you for your attention.

For such wartime broadcasts on German radio Joyce was given the *Kriegsverdienstkreuz* [war service cross] by Hitler, the mock title "Lord Haw-haw" by the British press and a death sentence by a British jury at the end of the war. Joyce was an outsider all his life. He was born in New York in 1906, the son of an Irish father and English mother who moved to Galway in 1914. There he went to school and later studied English at London university. A false claim to be a British citizen in order to secure a passport was to have dramatic consequences. Joyce first joined the Conservative party, then became a member of Mosley's fascists and finally formed his own National Socialist League. An admirer of the Nazis, he went to Germany with his second wife just before the war broke out in 1939. There he gave the broadcasts which made his name a household word in Britain (and in Ireland). Hitler's defeat ended all his hopes and he was captured by a British soldier while attempting to cross over the border into Denmark. Joyce was betrayed by his unmistakable radio voice. Ironically the lie about his place of birth later ensured he was charged with treason, found guilty and hanged on 3 January 1946.

THE ELEVEN-YEAR-OLD UNIVERSITY STUDENT

William Thompson, Baron Kelvin of Largs
(1824-1907)

In 1835 an eleven-year-old boy was enrolled as an undergraduate at the university of Glasgow. He was later to
become professor of natural philosophy at his old college at
the age of twenty-two and remained an important figure in
science for the next fifty-three years. His statue stands at the
entrance to Botanic Park in Belfast because he was born in
that city and as he became one of the most famous scientists
of the nineteenth-century the city was glad to claim him as
a native son. He was born on 26 June 1824, the son of the

head of mathematics at the Royal Belfast Academical Institution. When his father was appointed professor of mathematics in Glasgow, Kelvin, a gifted child, very soon passed the matriculation and became an undergraduate. During his career he published over 600 scientific papers and by the time of his death was entitled to write more academic degrees after his name than any man then alive. Out of his research into conservation of energy he discovered the Second Law of Thermodynamics and he also devised a more accurate way of determining the age of the earth. His work on electrical currents enabled the Atlantic cable to be laid after many previous failures. This earned him a knighthood in 1866. He was too an inventor of many useful scientific devices including a compass which was adopted by the Royal Navy, a tide-measurer for harbours and a depth-sounder which played its part in the cable-laying. He was very skilful manually and made the prototypes for his inventions in his own workshop, and was also a keen yachtsman. He was created Baron Kelvin of Largs in 1892 and received the Order of Merit ten years later. His fame is perpetuated in that his name was given to the standard measure of temperature on the Kelvin scale. He died on 17 December 1907.

THE FIRST ARCHBISHOP

St. Laurence O'Toole (1132 -1180)

The patron saint of Dublin was born in Castledermot in
1132. When he was a young boy he was sent as a hostage to
the court of Diarmuid Mac Murrough, the execrated king of
Leinster, who is blamed for the coming of the Normans to
Ireland. He was eventually rescued and sent for education
to the monastery of Glendalough. Here he proved so clever
and virtuous that he was made abbot in 1157 when he was
still only twenty-five. Meanwhile the city of Dublin was
growing. It had been made an archbishopric in 1152 and the
citizens felt that they were entitled to an archbishop. The

119

young abbot was the unanimous choice of clergy and people and he was consecrated in 1167. During the next nine years he ruled the city and church under the protection first of Diarmuid MacMurrough and later of Rory O'Connor, king of Connacht, who drove Diarmuid out. In 1170 the Normans came. At first Laurence organised resistance but when Rory was defeated by Strongbow, the Norman leader, he determined to sue for peace and accepted, on behalf of his flock, Strongbow's rule. He persuaded the Norman leader to build what was in fact a new cathedral, Christ Church. He continued to act as a go-between for Gael and Gall though he was not trusted by Henry II of England. He died on a diplomatic mission at Eu, in Normandy on 14 November 1180. He is one of only two canonised Irish saints.

THE PRAGMATIST

Seán Lemass (1899-1971)

The republicans who had lost the argument about the Treaty should forget "abstruse points about a *de jure* this or a *de facto* that and form a new party to win elections." The delegates to the meeting, held on Good Friday 1926, listened with respect to Seán Lemass, the young Dubliner (born 15 July 1899) whose credentials were impeccable. He had served in the Volunteers under de Valera,* had been in the GPO in 1916, had fought in the Anglo-Irish war and then in the Four Courts with those who rejected the treaty. They were persuaded by his arguments and so began the Fianna

Fáil party which came to power after the 1932 election. The Taoiseach Eamon de Valera made Lemass his industry and commerce minister, a job he was to fill in every Fianna Fáil government until he succeeded Dev as taoiseach in 1959. In the 1930s he followed Griffith's policy of protecting native industry by government involvement, setting up such semi-state bodies as Bórd na Móna, Aer Lingus, Irish Life Insurance and the Irish Tourist Board. During the 1939-45 "Emergency," Lemass had even greater power as the man in charge of supplies for a neutral Ireland. Protectionism was no longer appropriate in the 1950s, so he changed to a policy of economic planning, encouragement of foreign investment and free trade, first with Britain and then with the EEC. As taoiseach of a newly prosperous republic in the 1960s he had talks with Terence O'Neill, the N. Ireland premier, in the hope that economics would bring the two parts of Ireland closer together. A man whose work was his life, he had scarcely retired before he died on 11 May 1971. He is remembered for a pragmatism which won Fianna Fáil just as many elections as de Valera's idealism.

THE LION OF ST JARLATH'S

John MacHale (1791-1881)

When you look around most Irish towns two buildings stand out, the Catholic church and the convent school. With their Gothic spires and arches and their robust stonework, they remain a monument to the nineteenth-century Irish people who built them. Their church, which had survived conquest and penal laws, had come at last into its own. Of the men who led this Catholic renaissance, two stand out: Paul Cullen, cardinal archbishop of Dublin, and John MacHale, archbishop of Tuam.

John MacHale was born in a poor, still Irish-speaking

area of Co Mayo. He was the first modern Irish Catholic bishop to be educated entirely at home, in a local hedge-school and at Maynooth. As a bishop he encouraged preaching in Irish and he himself made a translation of the *Pentateuch* and of the catechism. He was a keen supporter of Daniel O'Connell*'s campaign for Catholic emancipation, encouraging his clergy to join. He continued to be a nationalist all his life, unlike Paul Cullen, whose long stay in Rome had made him very suspicious of revolutionary movements. MacHale agreed with Cullen on the need for a Catholic educational system at all levels but objected to the appointment of Newman, an Englishman, as head of the new Catholic university. Cullen who was younger but had greater influence in Rome won the power-struggle and with it a cardinal's red hat. But MacHale lived on to his ninetieth year in the precincts of the great cathedral and schools he had built in Tuam. In the battle to be remembered in popular tradition, the "Lion of St Jarlath's" has won hands down.

THE MEN AT THE GATE

Micheál MacLiammóir (1899-1978) and
Hilton Edwards (1903-82)

Dublin's Abbey Theatre is famous all over the world but
there was a time in the Thirties and Forties when its fame
was eclipsed by the Gate, a theatre run by two remarkable
men, one Irish, Micheál MacLiammóir, and one English,
Hilton Edwards. MacLiammóir was born Michael Wilmer
in Cork on 25 October 1899 and became a child actor in the
London theatre. He studied art at the Slade and toured
Europe as a painter before coming to Ireland to become a
member of his brother-in-law Anew McMaster's touring

125

company. He had joined the Gaelic League in London and become a fluent Irish speaker. His diaries, which were published from time to time, were written in Irish.

Edwards was born in London in 1903 and became an actor, theatre director and innovatory stage electrician. He and his fellow-actor met on tour in 1927 and by 1930 they had set up the Gate Theatre in Parnell Square in Dublin. They produced, not without controversy, the best of modern European and classical plays. They also staged modern Irish plays such as Denis Johnston's *The Old Lady Says "No"* at a time when the Abbey seemed to have lost heart. Both acted, and MacLiammóir's exotic stage sets were lit brilliantly by Edwards. MacLiammóir achieved international fame with his one-man show *The Importance of Being Oscar* which he played regularly from 1960 till 1975. He was Iago in the underrated film of Shakespeare's *Othello*, made by the one-time Gate actor, Orson Welles. MacLiammóir died on 6 March 1978 having written in his time ten plays and nine books about his life in the theatre. Edwards died on 18 November 1982.

THE FIRST WOMAN WHO…

Constance Gore-Booth,
Countess Markievicz (1868-1927)

Who was the first woman to be elected to the British House of Commons? Who was the first woman to be elected as deputy to the Dáil? Who was the first woman Minister of Labour ever? And who was the first woman to wave a pistol on the steps of the hotel in Kilrush? They were all the same woman, Con Gore-Booth, and those who knew her when she was a girl in Co Sligo would not have been at all surprised. For she always felt the need to do great deeds.

She was born in London on 4 February 1868, educated

by a governess in the family home at Lissadell, Co Sligo, and the year she "came out," "the new Irish beauty" became the toast of London and Dublin society. While studying art at the famous Julian School in Paris she met Count Dunin-Markievicz, a Polish Catholic nobleman with a dying wife. His adoption of Ireland as a second home caused Padraic Colum to remark that the only stage Irishman he ever met was a Pole. When his wife died, Casimir was free to marry Constance Gore-Booth and the ceremony took place in 1900. Their only child, Maeve, was reared by her grandmother at Lissadell.

Constance became friendly with Yeats,* whom she had known as a neighbour in Sligo, and was involved with both the Gaelic League and the Irish Literary Revival, though in spite of being otherwise an accomplished linguist, she, like her companion-in-arms, Roger Casement,* found Irish too difficult to learn. In 1906 she became interested in Sinn Fein and in 1909 developed Bulmer Hobson's idea of an Irish boy-scout brigade and formed *Na Fianna*, the youth movement of the IRB. She was herself a magnificent horsewoman and a crack shot and the young men of *Na Fianna* got excellent training in the use of arms. During the 1913 lock-out and general strike she ran a soup-kitchen in Dublin and was second-in-command to Michael Mallin in the College of Surgeons during the Easter Rising. She was condemned to death but released under the general amnesty of 1917. Shortly afterwards she became a Catholic. She was elected MP for St Patrick's division, Dublin and in the first Dáil Eireann which met in January 1919 she was made Minister of Labour. She was active during the War of Independence and opposed the Treaty. Like several other Republicans imprisoned by Free State forces she went on hunger strike. She joined Fianna Fáil in 1926 and was elected to the Dáil in 1927 but she died in Dublin on 15 July of that year. Casimir, who had not been in Ireland since 1913, came from Warsaw to be at her bedside.

THE MEDICAL MISSIONARY

Mother Mary Martin (1892-1975)

The International Missionary Training Hospital at Drogheda was *en fête* in 1962; among the distinguished guests were the patriarch of Armenia and Cardinal Montini (later Paul VI). A great army of white-habited doctors and nurses were celebrating the twenty-fifth anniversary of the founding of their order, the Medical Missionaries of Mary. The visitors from Rome were being guided around the gathering by the diminutive figure of Mary Martin, the Mother-general. Born the eldest of twelve children of a wealthy Dublin timber-merchant, she was educated by the

Sacred Heart nuns in Leeson Street and was later a boarder at Harrogate in England. During the 1914-18 war she worked as a nurse in France, afterwards returning to Dublin to do midwifery at Holles Street hospital. She had decided to devote her life to the sick, and so set out for Nigeria to work for the Bishop of Calabar, Joseph Shanahan. She came to believe that dedicated medical missionaries could do enormous good among the poor and the sick. Shanahan, who had just helped found the Missionary Sisters of the Holy Rosary, sent her to them at Killeshandra. After two years she left, and there followed a period of ill-health. But she never lost faith in her idea, which she continually pressed on the Papal Nuncio, Paschal Robinson. In 1936 Pius XI announced that nuns could become doctors, and within a year Mary Martin had set up the Medical Missionaries of Mary (MMM) in Nigeria. Unable to remain in Africa because of her health, she returned to Ireland, there to establish a student house at Booterstown, a novitiate at Collon, and finally the maternity hospital at Drogheda which became the order's headquarters. By the time of the twenty-fifth anniversary, the MMM had hospitals in Africa, USA, Italy and Spain. Mary Martin's greatest achievement was to get the church to recognise the unique work which could be done by women religious as doctors. For this she was decorated both by the International Red Cross and the Royal College of Surgeons of Ireland before her death at Drogheda (27 January 1975).

THE APOSTLE OF TEMPERANCE

Fr Theobald Mathew (1790-1856)

In Ireland at the start of the nineteenth-century drink was very cheap and there was always plenty of home-distilled stuff available. The effect was to increase the wretchedness of life, especially among the poor of the cities. Sometimes whole families were addicts. Yet because of the work of one man, half the population of Ireland gave up drink. In the six years from 1838 to 1844 the government revenue from liquor fell from £1.4 to £0.8 million.

The man who accomplished all this was Theobald Mathew. He was born at Thomastown Castle, Cashel in Co

Tipperary on 10 October 1790. His father was land-agent to Lord Llandaff. He went to Maynooth to study for the priesthood in 1807 but soon left to join the Capuchin fathers. He was sent to minister to the poor of Cork city where he found it necessary to set up free schools and welfare schemes and to lay out a new cemetery for his wretched flock. His work during the cholera epidemic of 1832 was regarded as heroic. In 1836 he was approached by an interdenominational group of philanthropists: the Rev N Dunscombe, a Church of Ireland clergyman, Richard Dowden, a Unitarian layman, and Billy Mack, a Quaker. They wished him to establish a total abstinence society. He led the way with his famous declaration on 10 April that year, "Here goes in the name of God." His work as a preacher against the evils of drink was all the more notable in that some of his close friends were distillers and brewers. He preached temperance in Britain and America with great success but needed a public subscription to rescue him from the debts incurred in the setting up of temperance clubs and reading rooms at home in Ireland. The journalist S C Hall found him a Civil List pension and he retired to Queenstown to live with his brother. He was a little bit disappointed at not being made Bishop of Cork but his health was not really up to the work. Father Mathew died on 8 December 1856, having been prematurely senile for some time.

THE RELUCTANT NUN

Catherine McAuley (1778-1841)

The order of the Sisters of Mercy, the largest religious community in the English-speaking world, owes its existence to three Dublin houses, Stormanstown House (now demolished) at Ballymun, Coolock House and the house in Baggot Street that became the first Mercy convent. The young lady who became the first Mercy sister did not really want to found an order or become a nun herself but because of the religious politics of the Dublin of her time there was no other way for her to do the work she wished, of educating young girls, of protecting the morals of older ones and of nursing the sick poor. Catherine McAuley was born in Stormanstown House on 29 September 1778 of moderately rich parents. Her father died when she was five and her mother who was easily influenced by rich friends lost all her money and her religion. When she died Catherine was twenty and was adopted by William and Catherine Callahan of Coolock House, a Quaker couple, who loved and respected her but tried to make her give up "Romish practices." William Callahan had, however, become a Catholic by the time of his death in 1822 and he left Catherine his house and fortune. It was while she lived in Coolock that she began to understand how much work needed to be done to alleviate the misery of the village poor, to say nothing of the conditions in the nearby city. Advised by local priests she built a "house of mercy" in Baggot Street. The women who helped her were to be free to give up the work when they felt inclined to do so but she decided, for reasons of continuity and to counter the clerical opposition she met at every turn, to formalise her community. Her Order of Mercy was established in 1835 but it was difficult for the rich, fifty-year-old woman to undergo the discipline of novitiate training. The order was finally approved by Pope Gregory XVI five months before its founder's death on 10 November 1841. By then there were ten convents in Ireland and two in England (in London and Birmingham). Since then the order has spread worldwide and with 23000 sisters it is the largest congregation of women in the church. The process for the canonisation of its remarkable founder is well advanced.

REVOLUTIONARY SON

Seán MacBride (1904-88)

The most colourful career in twentieth-century Ireland
culminated in the winning of the Nobel and Lenin peace
prizes. Even its beginnings were out of the ordinary for
Seán MacBride was the son of a revolutionary father,
executed after the 1916 rising, and a revolutionary mother,
Maud Gonne. A Parisian by birth and education, his voice
always retained a French inflection. As a member of the IRA
he opposed in turn the British, the majority who accepted
the limited independence of 1922, and those who set up
Fianna Fáil and took power in 1932. Eventually he became

chief-of-staff of what remained of the IRA. At the same time he made his living as a journalist for Parisian and London newspapers. He also became a barrister and even after he had left the IRA he continued to defend republican prisoners. The Clann na Poblachta party he had set up formed part of the coalition government of 1948-51 in which he was foreign minister. He was a major influence in the decision to stay out of NATO and leave the Commonwealth. When his political career ended he served as chairman of Amnesty International (1961-74), which he had helped found. The UN asked him to serve as commissioner in Namibia and later as chairman of a UNESCO commission on communications. Finally his interest moved from the world stage back to his own country, when he tried to persuade US firms in the North to follow the "MacBride principles" and positively discriminate to redress Catholic disadvantage. The venerable revolutionary died at his home in Clonskeagh on 15 January 1988 and was buried in the republican plot at Glasnevin.

THE GREAT TENOR

John McCormack (1884-1945)

One evening at a posh dinner-party in New York two
distinguished guests were pleased to entertain the
company. First the great composer Rachmaninov played
the piano; then he was asked to accompany the great
concert tenor. The tenor sang an operatic aria and then a
popular Irish song. When it was over Rachmaninov said
with a smile, "John, you sing a good song well but you sing
a bad song magnificently."

The tenor, John McCormack, was born in Athlone on 14
June 1884 and made his operatic debut in *Cavalleria*

Rusticana at Covent Garden in 1907. He later appeared in *La Traviata* (Manhattan Opera House, 1909). He had a superb voice with remarkably clear diction but he admitted to being embarrassed by the acting required for operatic roles. After a number of opera seasons, including a tour of Australia with Dame Nellie Melba, he abandoned the stage and became a concert performer. He was immediately hailed as the greatest lyric tenor of the age. He made more than 500 recordings and gave concerts all over the world except in South America and Russia. He became an American citizen in 1919 but kept houses in Ireland, in Monasterevin and Booterstown and he was created a hereditary papal count because of his great services to charity. He died on 16 September 1945 in his Booterstown home. For a whole generation he was, in every sense, the voice of Ireland.

BELFAST'S RADICAL DAUGHTER

Mary Ann McCracken (1770-1866)

The name of Mary Ann McCracken has been eclipsed by that of her more colourful brother. This seems unfair since he died young and had little success in the activities in which he was engaged, whereas Mary Ann lived a long life and was much more successful in anything she attempted. Born into a family of linen merchants, she attended an early coeducational school run by David Manson. She was especially good at figures, an attribute that stood her in good stead when with her sister she set up their own muslin business. She believed passionately that "if woman was created as a companion for man she must, of course, be his equal in understanding." So she involved herself in the collection of old Irish harp music which had been begun by Edward Bunting.* She was enthusiastic about the revolutionary changes in France and worked for similar change in Ireland. She was a good friend of Thomas Russell (and through him, of Wolfe Tone*) and she encouraged them to organise a society of United Irishmen to bring about change. When her beloved brother Harry who had become a "United man" was arrested (by a government fearful of revolution) she visited him and wrote to him all through his year (1796) in Kilmainham gaol. In 1798 she realised that there was very little hope of a successful revolution but she suppported Harry in his necessary involvement. When he was defeated at Antrim and captured, she attended his trial, and afterwards "took his arm and we walked together to the place of execution." On his death she took care of his illegitimate daughter, Maria. In 1803 she supported Thomas Russell when he was tried for treason and afterwards paid for a flagstone for his grave. In later life she was the secretary of the Belfast Charitable Society and here she showed her enlightened ideas about the treatment of the poor. Her last years were spent helping Dr Madden to write his history of the United Irishmen as she, in her nineties, was one of the few still alive who had been involved. In the end she died still faithful to the Presbyterian radicalism of her native city. In the history books the brother she knew as "Harry" is called Henry Joy McCracken, the hero of 1798. She is rarely mentioned.

THE LITTLE FENIAN

Alice Milligan (1865-1953)

There was once a little Protestant girl whose Protestant
nurse warned her that the Fenians would get her if she did
not come when she was called. This little girl was quite a
rebel and thought, "When the Fenians come I'll go after."
She was Alice Milligan and for all of her life she was a
vigorous republican. She was born in September 1865, the
daughter of Seaton F Milligan, a wealthy Omagh
businessman and antiquary. She was educated at
Methodist College, Belfast, Magee College, Derry and
King's College, London but turned down an offer to go to

Germany to learn German and opted instead to go to Dublin to learn Irish. The year of her thirty-third birthday was the centenary of the 1798 rising and she was organising secretary for the northern celebrations. She wrote a life of Wolfe Tone* for the centenary and later became interested in the Irish Literary Theatre, the precursor of the Abbey. Her play *The Last Feast of the Fianna* was produced at the Gaiety Theatre with music by her sister Charlotte, who was an authority on Irish folk music. She was also involved in the first ever use of Irish on stage, in a tableau about St Patrick at Tara which was presented at Aonach Tír Chonaill at Letterkenny in November 1898. During her active political life she lived in Belfast and edited in partnership with her friend Anna Johnston (Ethna Carbery) the literary and political journal, the *Sean Van Vocht*. She was a leading member of Arthur Griffith*'s Sinn Féin and a friend of James Connolly.* She died at Tyrcar, Omagh, on 13 April 1953.

THE MINSTREL BOY

Thomas Moore (1779-1852)

In Regency drawing rooms throughout London, the songs
that were fashionable were not the latest *chansons* from
Paris or *Lieder* from Weimar but airs about wild harps and
collars of gold and minstrel boys. Romantic Ireland was all
the rage and ladies who hardly knew where Dublin was
sang soulfully about Lir's lonely daughter telling "to the
night-star her tale of woes." The cause of this hibernic-
isation was a poet with a fine tenor voice and a lovely Irish
accent that was really an English one with Irish vowels. In
his way and at that time he was Ireland's best ambassador,

and though his songs seemed to be set safely in the past they had relevance to her contemporary situation. Tom Moore never forgot nor let anyone else forget that he was Irish and never neglected an opportunity to remind his English friends of Ireland's wrongs.

He was born in 12 Aungier Street on 28 May 1779. His father was a prosperous grocer from Kerry and his mother a bright and vigorous Wexford lass. He received a good education and was one of the first Catholics to be admitted to Trinity College. There he met Robert Emmet* but though he agreed with his view of an independent Irish nation he did not become a United Irishman. When Emmet was executed after his abortive rising in 1803 Moore wrote two songs, one for him, "O Breathe Not His Name," and a second for his sweetheart, Sarah Curran, "She Is Far From the Land." In London he gave up his legal studies to live on sinecures and on money earned from poetry which ranged from the erotic to the oriental. He was a good amateur actor and his wife Bessie Dyke was an actor. He almost fought a duel with Francis Jeffrey, the editor of *The Edinburgh Review*, because it had declared some of his poems immoral but when they met the two men became good friends; he nearly fought a duel with Lord Byron and they became even better friends. He made a lot of money from his oriental verse romance *Lalla Rookh* but his reputation depends on the Irish Melodies that had established his fame.

He died on 25 February 1852 in Sloperton Cottage which had been his home in Wiltshire for thirty-five years. He was suffering from Alzheimer's syndrome, a condition aggravated by the sad fact that all of his five children had predeceased him. Yet he lives still wherever his Melodies are sung with his words carefully fitted to older Irish airs.

THE WILD IRISH GIRL

Sydney Owenson, Lady Morgan
(?1776-1859)

No one knows for certain when she was born. One story is that the event occurred on Christmas Day, 1776, halfway across the Irish Sea during a storm. Her mother was English, her father an actor-manager and fine singer from Co Mayo. He had been born MacOwen but changed his name to Owenson to reassure English management and dropped his Catholic religion to make certain of a career. He was unsuccessful as a theatre manager in Dublin, Kilkenny, Derry and Sligo. His eldest daughter, who had received some education at Clontarf, became a governess. Like her near contemporary, Tom Moore,* she published some "Hibernian Melodies" which were fashionable with London society at the time. She drew upon her Irish-speaking relatives and the Mayo home of her father to write her best seller, *The Wild Irish Girl* (1806). Sydney Owenson was taken up by the Marchioness of Abercorn and married on her instruction the family surgeon, Charles Morgan, who was given a knighthood as a wedding present. It was then, as Lady Morgan, that Sydney began to hold a literary salon in her house in Kildare Street, Dublin. Her books were romantic with much artificial "Irishness" that pleased English readers. She became a great traveller and published books about her adventures which became as popular as her novels. Lady Morgan remained an active nationalist and supporter of Catholic emancipation, and was the first woman to receive a pension for her services to literature. By the time she died in London on 16 April 1859, she had become a very rich woman and was able to leave money for benevolent funds for actors and governesses.

GOD'S BEGGAR

Nano Nagle (1718-1784)

In the last quarter of the eighteenth century a woman wrapped in a black cloak and carrying a lantern was often to be seen about the streets of Cork. Her purpose was twofold: to collect alms for the poor under her protection and to minister where she could to the sick and the old. So sweetly persistent was she in her alms-gathering that her benefactors called her "God's beggar" and she benefited her city as few others have done.

Nano Nagle was born in Balgriffin, near Mallow on the Blackwater, in 1718, the eldest child of Ann Mathew and

Garret Nagle, a prosperous landowner and merchant. She was christened Honoria but was universally called "Nano." Ireland was then in the grip of the Penal laws which were designed ostensibly to make Catholics become Protestant or suffer social and spiritual degradation. Catholic schools were forbidden and the poor children of Cork ran wild.

She was sent to France for her education but like many children from her district including, for a time, her kinsman Edmund Burke,* the great orator, she had attended the hedge-school in the ruins of Monanimy Castle, near Castletownroche. The social life of Paris nearly claimed her but, prompted by her sister Ann (b. 1722), she returned home after a period spent as a novice in a French convent.

She was twenty-six when she opened her first school for poor children in Cove Lane and by the time she decided to found the Order of the Presentation Sisters of the BVM she had established seven schools in the city. She and three companions, Mary Collins, Elizabeth Burke and Mary Tuohy, pronounced their final vows before Bishop Moylan on 24 June 1777.

By the date of her death on 26 April 1784 her order, with its rule which "excluded every exercise of charity which was not in favour of the poor," was well established. It has since spread to England, America, Australia and India.

FEAR AN ASAIL BHIG DHUIBH

Padraic Ó Conaire (1882-1928)

In 1928 a man died in the Richmond Hospital in Dublin and the only possessions he had were a pipe, a few ounces of tobacco and an apple. The man was Padraic Ó Conaire and if you go to his native city of Galway you will see his memorial statue in Eyre Square. It shows him with hat, stick and walking-boots, looking like a wise old leipreachán. He was a writer, one of the finest in modern Irish, and his best-known book, *M'Asal Beag Dubh*, describes his journeyings about Ireland.

He was born in 1882 at 5 High Street, Galway but from

the age of eleven he was brought up in Connemara by his grandparents, his parents having died. When he was fifteen he went to Rockwell and later Blackrock College with the intention of becoming a priest but changed his mind and joined the Ministry of Education in London as a clerk. He became a Gaelic League teacher in London and is the subject of a story that might not be apocryphal. For a promotion examination he offered Irish among other subjects. The examining board got in touch with the Gaelic League asking them to set and mark an Irish paper of the appropriate standard for their clerk, Patrick Conroy. The Gaelic League teacher, Padraic Ó Conaire, was only too pleased to do it for the fee but finding a mistake in a *síneadh fada* only gave Patrick Conroy 99 per cent.

By 1914 he had won two Oireachtas prizes for works in Irish. He resigned from his post, came back to Ireland and began the wandering, writing life that he followed till his death. His stories, *Deoraidheacht* (1910), *An Chéad Chloch* (1914) and *Scothscéalta* are still in print. They are based on fact and full of the drama of real life, sometimes wildly comic, sometimes starkly tragic.

He was a man in love with Ireland and his chosen life. In the final sentence of *M'Asal Beag Dubh* (here in translation) he bids farewell to his donkey and the roads of Banba (as he calls his country) at the coming of inhospitable winter. It gives us a good idea of his style and freshness of language:

> O, noble clans of the roads of Banba, I bid you farewell for a while until the sky clears, until biting winter passes away, until the golden, sultry summer comes again—a genial, pleasant Irish summer—farewell.

151

THE ISLANDMAN

Tomás Ó Criomhthain (1856-1937)

"Cá'il an sneachta bhí có geal anurig?"

[Where is the snow that was so bright last year?]

I sprang up in excitement and cried out: *"Où sont les neiges d'antan?"*

"Who said that?" asked the King, an expert in this lore.

"Francois Villon said it," I replied.

"And who was he," he returned. "Was he a Connachtman?"

"No, he lived hundreds of years ago and he said it in French, and it was a proverb of his people."

"Well," broke in Tomás, "You can't better the proverb. I've always heard that the French are a clever people, and I wouldn't put it past them to have said that before we did."

So Robin Flower, one of many scholarly visitors to the island, remembered an evening in the Blascaod Mór. The scholars who came to the island to learn Irish, in turn encouraged the islanders to write of their lives. Two autobiographies were great successes, *Peig* by Peig Sayers* and *Fiche Bliain ag Fás* by Muiris Ó Súilleabháin. But the best book of all was written by the Tomás of Flower's story. Published in 1929 as *An tOileánach*, it tells of Ó Críomhthain's schooldays, of his first trip to the mainland, of working as a fisherman and on a small farm, of marrying and becoming the father of ten children. He describes learning to read his own language from children at school in Dún Chaoin, where Irish was being taught in the area for the first time. He records especially his delight when Carl Marstrander, a great scholar come to learn Irish, called him by the title of "*máistir*." Tomás wrote of his reasons for writing, "*chun go mbeadh ár dtuairisc 'ar ndiaidh, mar ná beidh ár leithéidí arís ann*" [to leave our story after us because there will not be our like again.] Sixteen years after his death the last islanders moved to the mainland.

AN FILE DEIREANNACH

Aogán Ó Rathaille (1670-c.1728)

Aogán Ó Rathaille has been the victim of the most awful fate
that can befall a poet: most of his countrymen can no longer
read his poems. While nearly everyone has some few lines
of Yeats* by heart, hardly a one knows of the man who was
probably our greatest poet before Yeats. Ó Rathaille may
well have foreseen his fate, for he lived through the final
dispossession of the old Irish families and the coming of
their English replacements. This cataclysmic event drove
him to his finest poetry, lamenting the passing of the old
Gaelic order and with it the slow death of the language in

154

which he wrote.

Born on a 250-acre farm in the Sliabh Luachra area of Co Kerry in 1670, Ó Rathaille was educated at one of the big houses of the great MacCarthy clan, where he studied Latin, old Irish manuscripts and English. He was one of the last of those who tried to live wholly by writing, like the old *filí*. He wrote poems in praise of the MacCarthys and the Brownes who were his patrons. After 1690 his favourite poetic form was the "aisling" in which the poet dreams of the restoration of the Stuarts and with them the old Gaelic, Catholic way of life. Finally he wrote the great bitter lament *"Cabhair ní ghairfead"* which ended:

> *Stadfadsa feasta—is gar dom éag gan mhoill*
> *ó treascadh dragain Leamhan, Léin is Laoi;*
> *rachad 'na bhfasc le searc na laoch don chill*
> *na flatha fá raibh mo shean roimh éag do Chríost.*

> [I'll not ask for help; it's soon I'll die,
> For the great of Leamhan, Léin and Laoi are defeated.
> My cerements about me, I'll join my chief in the grave,
> With those who ruled before Christ's sacrifice.]

On his death which occurred around 1728 he joined his great patron: both are buried in Muckross Abbey in Killarney.

THAT LADY

Kate O'Brien (1897-1974)

Like all good writers Kate O'Brien wrote about what she knew best, her own life. She was born into a bourgeois Limerick family whose ancestors had come penniless to the city from famine-ridden Clare (much as did the characters in her first novel *Without My Cloak* (1931). Her mother died when she was six and she went as a boarder to the Faithful Companions of Jesus Convent at Laurel Hill. In *The Land of Spices* (1941) she gives a wonderfully observed picture of convent life from both pupil's and nun's points of view. Long summer holidays in a lodge in Kilkee are lovingly recalled. After graduation from UCD she was in turn a journalist in London and a secretary to her uncle who represented the new revolutionary Dáil of 1919 in Washington. Then she went to Spain and began a life-long love-affair with that country. She set her famous historical novel *That Lady* (1946) there. In *Mary Lavelle* (1936), also set in Spain, the young Irish governess and the son of the house fall in love, but as he is married she knows the affair will be temporary. Kate O'Brien herself married in 1924 but it was not a success and she and her husband soon parted. The novel *As Music and Splendour* (1958) which tells of the adventures of two Irish girl singers in Italy and of the love affair of one of them with a Spanish soprano may give a clue as to the cause of the parting. Between 1939 and 1945 she lived in London and wrote *The Last of Summer* (1943), its theme a Franco-Irish love affair set on the eve of the war. As always she writes of Limerick, of the Clare coast, of Ireland's connection with Catholic Europe, of religious feeling, of the lives of women (and men) and of love. Her last years were spent in England after a happy but improvident decade at Roundstone in the 1950s. Her work is still very readable both for her descriptions of an Irish Catholic bourgeois past which is now a fading memory, and for her account of the life of the emotions which has a universal appeal.

THE CATHOLIC EMANCIPIST

Daniel O'Connell (1775-1847)

To recount O'Connell's career is to recount much of the history of Ireland, of Britain and indeed of Europe at the time. He was born on 6 August 1775 into a prosperous Kerry family with a tradition of military service to the kings of France, and his education at Douai was interrupted by the French revolutionaries' suspicion of Catholic colleges. As a young barrister in Ireland, he was convinced by the cruel repression of the 1798 rebellion that violence was not the way to bring about change. But change there had to be, in a country where a Protestant minority looked to the union with Britain to keep them in power over the much-feared mass of Catholics, and at a time when the French revolution had made the coming of democracy inevitable. Realising this, O'Connell formed a radical Catholic Association to collect money from the masses in order to finance election campaigns. In this way he became the first Catholic MP (illegally, for Clare in 1828); then forced the British government to allow Catholics to sit in parliament, and by 1832 had a party of thirty-nine Irish MPs advocating the repeal of the union and the return of a parliament to Ireland. Throughout the 1830s he supported the Whig policy of liberal reform. However, when the Tories came to power in Britain, people in Ireland began to desert him and support the more radical demands of the Young Irelanders. His last years were saddened by this loss of influence and by the awfulness of the famine which engulfed the country in the mid-1840s. Already ill, he set out for Westminster to speak for famine aid and went thence to Rome where he wished to spend his last days. He died in Genoa on 15 May 1847 but his heart completed the journey, to be preserved in the *Collegio irlandese.* His body lies in a vault in Glasnevin cemetery under a memorial in the shape of a great round tower, the most striking monument in all the ground.

O'Connellism confirmed later Irish Protestants in their belief that they could not live in an independent Ireland. On the other hand British radicals accepted him as a valuable ally in the struggle for democratic change. Above all the mass of the Catholic poor adored him as the first Catholic Irishman to plead successfully for them politically. And all of literary Europe accepted Balzac's judgement: *"O'Connell fut grand parce qu'il incarna un peuple entier."*

THE PRIDE OF THE COOMBE

Jimmy O'Dea (1899-1965)

Between 1924 and 1965 the audiences in Dublin theatres often found themselves in stitches at the antics of a qualified optician dressed as a lady-fruitseller using dialogue written by an ex-house-painter. Jimmy O'Dea was born in Dublin in 1899 and qualified as an oculist in Edinburgh. He acted in amateur productions of Ibsen and Chekhov but became a full-time comedian when he met Harry O'Donovan in the early Twenties. O'Dea-O'Donovan productions were a staple not only of the Dublin entertainment scene but also of the English music-halls and BBC radio in, during and after the 1939-45 war. O'Dea's most famous character was Biddy Mulligan, the vegetable-seller, though the song which became his signature-tune was originally sung by another performer. No pantomime or summer variety season was complete without this Dublin character. O'Dea was not so much a comedian as a brilliant actor who was capable of great pathos. He was small and incorrigibly genial with a voice of great subtlety and power. In the thirties he and O'Donovan made a number of records of their sketches which are still very funny. O'Dea also played in films. He began in the twenties with three Irish silent movies and in the thirties made a total of five comedies for Irish and British studios. His most famous parts were as the engine-driver in *One Minute Wait* (1957) and as the King of the Fairies in *Darby O'Gill and the Little People* (1959). He died on 7 January 1965.

THE BLUESHIRT

Éoin O'Duffy (1892-1944)

All over Europe in the 1920s and 1930s uniformed fascist organisations engaged in violence against communists, against Jews and against democracy. Italy and Germany became dictatorships. So when the Blueshirt movement began under Eoin O'Duffy in the early 1930s, some feared for democracy in Ireland. In fact democracy was in no danger from the Monaghan-born (30 October 1892) O'Duffy, who after service in the Anglo-Irish war was made chief of police by the government of the new Free State. As Gárda Síochána commissioner he was both efficient and

162

very independent. This latter quality did not endear him to de Valera* who became Taoiseach in 1932 and he was forced to resign. So O'Duffy became chief of the Army Comrades Association which had been set up to protect meetings of political parties opposed to Fianna Fáil from disruption by physical attack. O'Duffy renamed the organisation the National Guard and gave them their blueshirt uniform. He was so successful that he was made head of the new Fine Gael party which united those opposed to Fianna Fáil. But O'Duffy lacked political skill and lost control of both Fine Gael and the Blueshirts. From 1935 on he devoted more of his time to international fascist meetings, and to the organising of an Irish brigade to fight in Spain on the side of Franco in the civil war. O'Duffy feared communism (disguised in Ireland, he thought, as the IRA) but his corporatism was that of the papal encyclical "Quadragesimo Anno" rather than Mussolini's. And most people thought enough of the man not to object to a state funeral when he died on 30 November 1944.

THE GREAT NORTHERN EARL

Hugh O'Neill (1550-1616)

Many Irish visitors to Rome make their way to the beautiful old church of San Pietro in Montorio to find the stone which bears the inscription, *Hic quiescunt Ugonis Principis O'Neill ossa.* [Here are at rest the bones of Hugh, chief of the O'Neills]. They go to pay homage to a man whose career was incredibly eventful. Born in Dungannon in 1550 he was fostered by Sir Henry Sydney at Ludlow Castle and there taught both English and the new Protestantism. He returned to Ireland as Earl of Tyrone in 1568 and for some years seemed loyal to Queen Elizabeth but in 1595 he had

164

himself inaugurated as "The O'Neill" at Tullyhogue, the ancient site of clan rituals. The Crown representative at Newry was Marshal Bagenal who immediately had O'Neill proclaimed traitor. Bagenal had always hated O'Neill who had eloped with his daughter, Mabel and made her his third wife. This personal enmity grew into open hostility and resulted in the Nine Years War fought between the English and an Ulster alliance led by O'Neill and O'Donnell of Tír Chonaill. O'Neill defeated and slew Bagenal at the Battle of the Yellow Ford in 1598. He then made a fool of the Earl of Essex whom Elizabeth had sent to deal with him. Afterwards he made a progress through Ireland in the manner of the old *Ard Ríthe* and made a mockery of the queen's claim to rule. She then sent her best general Lord Mountjoy with a large army. Though he had Spanish help O'Neill was defeated at Kinsale and was forced to retreat to Ulster.

There he showed himself again an able diplomat and managed to obtain a pardon from Mountjoy and to retain possession of his lands. His powers were severely curtailed by the English and he was eventually persuaded by O'Donnell that their best hope was to spearhead a counter reformation attack on Ireland from Europe. This attack never came, for Spanish strength was in decline, and so O'Neill spent his last years in Rome in ineffectual negotations and in helping Archbishop Peter Lombard write his biography. The Archbishop naturally rendered him as fighting *pro fide Catholica*. Meanwhile at home in the Glen of Aherlow in Tipperary, Seathrún Céitinn in his *Foras Feasa ar Éirinn* was portraying O'Neill as the latest in a long line of those who had died "in defence of the Gael."

THE LAST MARTYR

St Oliver Plunkett (1625-1681)

In St Peter's Church in Drogheda there is a rather gruesome relic, the preserved head of a martyred saint. He was the last person to be executed for his faith on the public scaffold at Tyburn (now Marble Arch) in west London. His name was Oliver Plunkett and he was an Anglo-Irish Catholic who was loyal to the British crown. He was closely related to the Earls of Fingall and Roscommon and to Lord Dunsany of Louth. He was born on 1 October 1625 at Loughcrew, Co Meath, studied for the priesthood in Rome and was ordained in 1654. Because of the Cromwellian persecution in Ireland he was allowed to remain in the Irish College as lecturer in theology. The primatial see of Armagh became vacant in 1669 and Plunkett was consecrated archbishop in exile. He came to take up his duties at home in 1670 at a period of tolerance for Catholicism while the sympathetic Duke of Ormond was viceroy.

The Church, like the country, was in a bad way. Many of the Catholic landowners had lost their lands and had become guerillas, while the priests were disaffected and often drunken. Plunkett had to face resentment from the Franciscans, who had held out courageously during the persecutions, and a personal feud with the archbishop of Dublin, Peter Talbot. During the next three years before religious persecution broke out again, he established schools for children and seminaries for clerics and novices and gave great heart to the Church. For six years from 1673 till 1679 he had to live in hiding, dressed in lay clothes and in great poverty but still carrying on his work as the head of the Church. He was arrested in 1679 and tried for high treason but the process collapsed. Then in 1681 in London he was found guilty on the manifestly perjured evidence of two Franciscan renegades. He was hanged on 1 July 1681 and his body was then drawn and quartered. The process of canonisation was protracted. He was beatified in 1920 but not fully canonised till 1975.

THE UNCROWNED KING

Charles Stewart Parnell (1846-91)

The son of a Protestant landowner married to an anglophobe American, Parnell dominates the later, as O'Connell* did the earlier, nineteenth century. He was born in Avondale, Co Wicklow, on 27 June 1846. As with all such great figures an account of his life is more than just a sequence of events. One part of his multifold achievement was to convince the Fenian believers in physical force that parliamentary action *could* achieve results. He also persuaded the small farmers of the Land League to campaign not just for fair rents and land ownership but also for self-government. Finally he used his tightly-disciplined party of eighty-six MPs to force the British parliament to grant Home Rule for Ireland. However, ambiguity was of the essence of this achievement so Home Rule was never precisely defined. The real unifying factor in all the campaigns was the incredible personal influence Parnell exercised, an influence which continued until an error of judgement on his part led to his relationship with a married woman becoming public knowledge. The scandal shocked his British liberal allies and split his own party. Some members rejected a leader who gave public scandal while others supported him, come hell or high water. Parnell died soon after the split but his death did not end the controversy caused by his fall from power. Who can forget Joyce*'s description in *A Portrait of the Artist as a Young Man* of the family Christmas dinner disrupted by an argument about Parnell which ended with the cry from Mr Casey, "Poor Parnell! My dead king!"?

THE MAN OF FAITH

St Patrick (c.400–c.490)

St Patrick is honoured on 17 March with a great parade in
Dublin (and in New York). Adults wear shamrock and the
children badges showing a picture of the saint driving out
snakes from Ireland. This tradition dates from the
seventeenth century. Also on 17 March is made a
pilgrimage to Saul, Co Down, where Patrick is supposed to
have founded his first church, and to nearby Downpatrick,
where twelfth-century tradition said the saint was buried.
That so many traditions have grown up around the saint's
name, including the penitential pilgrimage to Lough Derg

in Co Donegal and the light-headed climb of Croagh Patrick on the last Sunday of July, is a tribute to the special place he holds in the hearts of the Irish people.

For the real saint we need to go to the eighth-century manuscript copy of the *Confessio* which Patrick himself wrote. In the awkward Latin (that of a man whose everyday language was now Gaelic) this son of Roman British parents tells of his capture, by the raiding party of an Irish chieftain at Boulogne-sur-mer, where his father was stationed. After working as a herdsman in Mayo and Antrim Patrick escaped to Gaul where he was educated under Germanus at Auxerre. He vividly describes hearing Mayo voices calling him in a dream: *"Rogamus te, sancte puer, ut venias et adhuc ambulas inter nos."* [We beg you, holy youth, come and walk amongst us again.] After being ordained bishop he set out in answer to the dream supplication and returned to the country of his servitude, where he was to stay for the rest of his life. It was to be a life given to prayer and the reading of the bible, to teaching, to spreading the Christian faith and to setting up churches and monasteries. It seems that Patrick worked mostly in Ulster and that is the chief reason that the ecclesiastical capital of Ireland is Armagh. Both great cathedrals there honour his name.

THE POET REVOLUTIONARY

Patrick H Pearse (1879-1916)

Patrick Pearse would like to have been remembered by the Gaelic version of his name for he was convinced that the most important symbol of nationality was language. The Dublin-born son of an English sculptor and an Irish mother, Pearse qualified as a barrister, but instead of practising he put all his energies into promoting the revival of Irish, as a member of the Gaelic League and editor of its newspaper *An Claidheamh Soluis*. With his brother Willy and Thomas McDonagh, he founded Sgoil Éanna in Rathfarnham, with the ideal of providing for boys an education that was Gaelic but also free of excessive academic restraints and pressures. Once when a parent complained to Pearse, "My son is no good at books, he is no good at work, he is no good at anything but playing the tin whistle," he replied, "Buy a tin whistle for him." He became interested in politics only in the years just before the outbreak of the 1914-1918 war, when like many other young men, he became disillusioned with the slow progress of the Irish Party and joined the Irish volunteers and the IRB. These republicans viewed the European war, "England's difficulty" as Ireland's opportunity. They chose Pearse to lead the rising they planned for Easter 1916. He read the *Proclamation of the Republic* and commanded the GPO garrison, but left the military tactics of the rising to James Connolly.* He remained dignified in surrender and was executed by firing squad shortly afterwards The deliberately sought martyrdom of Pearse and his devotion to the idea of blood-sacrifice led later historians to view him with mixed feelings. However, he can be unreservedly admired as an innovative educationalist and as the creator of a small body of lyric poetry and stories.

THE SHIPBUILDER

William James Pirrie (1847-1924)

Born in Quebec of Irish parents on 24 May 1847, Pirrie was
brought back to Ireland by his mother on the death of his
father. He might be said to epitomise all that was best in the
nineteenth-century Ulster: he worked hard, had a world-
view of industry and maintained his political
independence. His working life began when he was
apprenticed to shipbuilding at the Belfast firm of Harland
& Wolff. Within twelve years he was a partner and became
chairman in 1895. He promoted the design and engineering
innovations which led to the building of liners of 45,000 tons

174

like the *Olympic* which, owned by the White Star Line, dominated the shipping-lanes of the north Atlantic. He saw Belfast in the context of world shipbuilding and kept a country house near London, the more easily to entertain significant industrial and political figures. He was host to the Kaiser on his yacht at the Kiel regatta of 1912, and then sailed on to Denmark to inspect a ship fitted with the newly developed diesel-engine, the importance of which he immediately realised. He was to die (on 7 June 1924) on board ship while on a business trip to South America. Above all he was a typical Ulsterman in having an independent view of Irish politics (though he did accept a viscountcy in 1921). Reared in the non-subscribing Presbyterian radical tradition, he was a constructive unionist who praised Plunkett*'s cooperative movement and the Irish National Teachers Organisation's work for education. He would have been willing to contemplate a measure of Home Rule for Ireland but not protectionist independence which he thought would have been disastrous for Belfast industry. In the end he accepted, but only as second-best, partition and a seat in the N Ireland senate.

THE CREAMERY MAN

Horace Plunkett (1854-1932)

Horace Plunkett was born on 24 October 1854 into a Co.
Meath Protestant family, wealthy enough to sent him to
Eton and Oxford. After ten year's ranching in Wyoming he
returned in 1889 to an Ireland where the majority were
determined to win a form of independence from Britain
which they called Home Rule. A young man of Plunkett's
background and education was naturally a unionist. The
problem as he saw it was how to present unionism as more
than just sterile opposition to the majority demand. He
wrote the book, *Ireland in the New Century* (1904), to suggest

176

an answer: "Ireland must be recreated from within." Moral and economic regeneration were more important than political change, he believed. He began a movement to encourage the economic policy of Cooperation and was particularly successful in getting dairy farmers to set up their own cooperative creameries. He used his influence as MP for south Co Dublin to get the government to set up a department of agriculture of which he became the first administrator in 1899. His loyalty to unionism became suspect and he lost his parliamentary seat in 1900. In 1907 he was made permanent president of the Irish Agricultural Organisation Society with headquarters in Merrion Square. By 1916 he had become convinced that the only policy that might unite both nationalist and unionist was to declare Ireland a dominion of the British Empire like Canada. The idea was rejected by unionists who preferred partition and by republicans who burned down his house at Kilteragh during the civil war. His last years were spent serving the new state as a senator and working for the cooperative movement worldwide. He died in Surrey on 26 March 1932.

THE LADY IN THE GLASS TOWER

Sarah Purser (1848-1943)

One day in 1938 a lady in her ninetieth year was flown over the roof of her own home to inspect its condition. The pilot was Oliver St John Gogarty, the man James Joyce* called "Buck Mulligan" in *Ulysses* and the fabric-inspecting passenger was an artist, a portrait painter and patron of stained-glass design in Ireland. Sarah Purser was born in what was then called Kingstown, Co Dublin, on 22 March 1848, the daughter of a rich miller. His business failed and when he emigrated to America, Sarah and her mother moved to Dublin where Sarah began a career in art. She studied portraiture in Paris, and her paintings of Countess Markievicz* and her sister Eva Gore-Booth proved so popular that she received many more commissions. In her own witty words she "went through the British aristocracy like the measles." She earned a considerable amount of money from these commissions and judicious investment in Guinness shares made her a rich woman. She used this money to encourage Irish artists and organised an exhibition of the works of Jack B Yeats and Nathaniel Hone in 1901. In 1903 with the help and advice of Edward Martyn, one of the founders of the Abbey Theatre, she established a workshop for stained glass called *An Túr Gloine* in Upper Pembroke Street, Dublin. After the establishment of the Free State she persuaded her friend W T Cosgrave to adapt Charlemont House in Parnell Square as the Municipal Gallery. This left the way clear for the ending of the controversy about the pictures which had been collected by Sir Hugh Lane, Lady Gregory*'s nephew, and bequeathed to the city when it should have an appropriate gallery in which to house them. Sarah Purser died in Dublin on 7 August 1943.

THE MISSIONARY

Edel Quinn (1907-44)

Pierre Lanais, the young Frenchman for whom she worked as a secretary in Dublin, recalled "She was always smiling and Edel Quinn's smile was something to remember; it was something bright and frank, wholly attentive and understanding; it shed light around her." He had fallen in love with the Kanturk-born (14 September 1907) girl who was educated at Loreto schools in Clonmel and Enniscorthy and at secretarial school in Dublin, moves made necessary by the fact that her father was a banker. Lanais found her wonderful company and an elegant dancer. Under her influence he began to go to mass again, something he had not done since childhood. Then in answer to his proposal of marriage she said she intended being a Poor Clare nun. In fact tuberculosis made this impossible but on her discharge from a sanatorium eighteen months later she found fulfilment in the Legion of Mary. Frank Duff*'s organisation for lay Catholics was so successful that it expanded outside Ireland, and Edel Quinn went to Kenya as an envoy. She worked among the poor there and later in Mauritius where her French proved useful. She also read French and was influenced spiritually by the writings of Thérèse de Lisieux and of Louis-Marie de Montfort. Hard work and constant self-denial led to an early death on 12 May 1944. The Irish sisters at Nairobi who had cared for her honoured her with burial in the missionaries' cemetery, next to Bishop Shanahan, another great missionary to Africa.

PARNELL'S HEIR

John Redmond (1856-1918)

When the news of the occupation of the GPO in Dublin in 1916 by a group of armed men broke on the world it shattered John Redmond both personally and politically. Two years later he was dead and his policy was rejected by the majority of the Irish people who voted against the Irish parliamentary party. As an MP for Wexford, where he was born on 1 September 1856, he had been an ardent supporter of Parnell,* to the extent of going to gaol in 1888. When Parnell's disgrace split the Irish parliamentary party he led its Parnellite wing, and (after 1900) the reunited party.

Redmond and the party pinned their hopes on the British allowing Home Rule, with Ireland still part of the United Kingdom, but with an Irish parliament to deal with local matters. He had little success with his policy until 1905 when a new liberal government slowly accepted Redmond's arguments. By 1914 Home Rule had become law and Redmond had at last triumphed. It was, however, a hollow victory, for the Ulster unionist opposition, whose strength he had underestimated, had forced him to accept partition, and the coming of European war meant the postponement of Home Rule. Redmond supported the British recruiting drive and his brother died in the war. Disillusioned with Redmond's limited success, more "advanced" nationalists refused to help Britain in the war and instead wondered if the use of force might not achieve an independent republic. Under the pressure of the European war the pace of events was too fast for Redmond. Those who had supported him for so long as "leader of the Irish race" deserted him and his party for the younger men of Sinn Féin who promised more. He died on 6 March 1918 and was buried in Wexford.

THE IRISH CHRISTIAN BROTHER

Edmund Ignatius Rice (1762-1844)

In their schools some boys became great hurlers or Gaelic footballers. Boys from poor backgrounds were given an education which afterwards allowed them to reach positions of influence; others remembered only the harsh punishments which inhibited rather than promoted achievement. Some were given a love of Irish culture and history which stayed with them all their lives; others rejected what they felt was extreme nationalist indoctrination. The schools were run by men who were known by their pupils as "the brothers" (or sometimes "the monks"). Pupils learned their proper name from the badge on their copy-books: *Fratres Scholarum Christianarum de Hibernia*.

Edmund Ignatius Rice, the man who founded the Irish Christian Brothers, was born near Callan in Co Kilkenny on 1 June 1762, the son of a "strong" farmer. In 1778 he was apprenticed to the meat export business of his uncle Michael in Waterford and he inherited the business on his uncle's death. He married in 1785 but his wife died at the birth of their only child, a daughter. The loss was a turning point in his life.

He became interested in the poor of Waterford and opened a school for their children in a stable in New Street in 1802. He spent everything he had on the school and then he was joined by other men with the same mission and they opened their first proper school at Mount Sion. By the time he had started schools in Clonmel and Dungarvan, he and his band of brothers felt the time had come to take religious vows. Pope Pius VII permitted the establishment of the congregation in 1820. It spread rapidly: there were soon CB schools in Cork (1811), Dublin (1812), Thurles (1815), Limerick (1816) and Ennistimon (1824). Schools were established in Britain, the first at Preston in 1825, and later in Australia, America, South Africa and India. This colossal expansion took place when Rice was still superior-general of the order. He eventually resigned in 1838 and spent his last years at Mount Sion in Waterford, where he died on 29 August 1844.

THE REPUBLICAN SOCIALIST

Frank Ryan (1902-44)

The young man from Elton, Co Limerick, who was a student of Irish at UCD while the war between the IRA and the British was going on, was disillusioned with the outcome of the struggle. So he fought in the civil war against the majority of his fellow countrymen who accepted the treaty and was interned after the republican defeat. Later he refused to follow the majority of the republicans who set up the new political party, Fianna Fáil, and held out for a more socialist republicanism. Finally, believing that republicans should support any struggle against European fascism, in

1936 he led 200 Irishmen to Spain to fight in the international brigade on the Republican side against Franco in the Spanish civil war. Wounded at the battle of Jarama he wrote home, "If I died in Spain, I would die for human liberty as certainly—perhaps more certainly—than I would in Ireland today." Captured by the victorious falangists (as Franco's supporters were called) and sentenced to death, he was reprieved after de Valera appealed to Franco. He went to Germany to consider an offer from the *Abwehr*, the Nazi secret service, to send him home to Ireland to organise pro-German republicans there but the plan was abandoned and he spent the war among the small Irish community in Berlin. In 1943 his health began to fail and he died in a sanatorium on 10 June 1944. Thirty-five years later his remains were taken home for re-interment at Glasnevin Cemetery.

THE WILD GOOSE

Patrick Sarsfield (c. 1650-1693)

Tradition remembers Sarsfield as a great Irish military hero but in fact it is much more useful to see him as an example of the mercenary nature of soldiering in the seventeenth century. The son of an Old English father and a Gaelic mother, he was educated in a French military academy. He first served under the Duc de Luxembourg in the French campaign of 1672 in the Netherlands. When James II became king of England in 1685 Sarsfield served in his household cavalry and was involved in the battle of Sedgemoor, the last fought on English soil, against the Duke of Monmouth who on the accession had led an unsuccessful rebellion against the king. After helping to remodel the king's army he left for France when James was dethroned by William of Orange in 1688. Louis XIV of France gave James an army to invade Ireland and Sarsfield was one of his commanders. He drove the Williamites from Connacht but his abilities were not used at the Boyne save to escort the fleeing king. Later he had his most glorious moment when he blew up William's siege train and so saved Limerick. Though created Earl of Lucan the following year he was still only a subordinate commander and his inability to agree with St Ruth, the French commander, was partly responsible for the Jacobite defeats at Athlone and Aughrim. He attempted to defend Limerick again but had to surrender to the Williamite general, Ginkel, in September 1691. Afterwards he led the thousands of "wild geese" who preferred to serve France rather than remain in a defeated homeland. With the Irish brigade of Louis XIV's army he continued to fight against the Dutch-English-Spanish alliance, at the battles of Steinkirk, where he was decorated, and of Landen where he was mortally wounded on 23 July 1693. He was mourned by the Irish brigade who idolised their tall, handsome commander, by his wife and son, and by a succession of writers and musicians who immortalised his name.

PEIG

Peig Sayers (1873-1958)

Peig Sayers is known to thousands of Irish schoolgoers by
the opening lines of her autobiography, *Peig*: *"Seanbhean is
ea mise anois, a bhuil cos lei san uaigh is an chos eile ar a bruach."*
["I'm an old woman now, with one foot in the grave and the
other on its edge."] And indeed it is a story with more than
its fair share of sadness and death. Although Peg Sayers is
usually associated with the Great Blasket Island and, along
with Tomás Ó Criomthain* and Muiris Ó Súilleabáin makes
up the great triumvirate of Blasket autobiographical
writers, she was actually born on the mainland, at Baile

Bhiocáire near Dunquin. Her family was very poor, so she went into service in Dingle at the age of fourteen. After a number of years she returned home because of ill-health and a match was made for her with Pádraig Guithín, ("Peats Flint") a Blasket Islander. After her marriage she lived on the Blasket until 1953. She had ten children, all of whom either died or emigrated, and her husband died while still a relatively young man. The difficulty of making a living from the small acreage of arable land and the wild and treacherous Atlantic emerges vividly from the story of her life. By 1953 the hardship and isolation of island life were considered to be untenable and the population had greatly decreased because of emigration. The government resettled the island people on the mainland. Peig died in hospital in Dingle in 1958.

Peig Sayers had a great store of folktales and songs and entertained visitors to the island for many years. As well as *Peig*, she produced two other volumes of memoirs/reminiscences: *Macnamh Seanmhná* and *Beatha Pheig Sayers*.

THE ANTARCTIC EXPLORER

Sir Ernest Shackleton (1874-1922)

Between 24 April and 10 May 1915 six men in a one-masted half-decker boat called the *James Caird* sailed 800 miles through the roughest, coldest and most dangerous seas in the world. It was the Antarctic winter and the men were polar explorers led by an Irishman, Ernest Shackleton. It was a typical adventure in the exciting life of the Irish explorer. He was born at Kilkea, Co Kildare on 15 February 1874 and was brought up in Dublin. He became a merchant seaman and soon got his master's ticket. His desire for adventure led him to join Captain Scott's Antarctic expedition of 1901 and he enjoyed everything about it except the Royal Navy discipline and the personality of the leader. In 1907 his own Antarctic expedition came nearest to the South Pole, reaching a latitude of 88° 23′ S. It had been a very difficult expedition but on his return home the British public made him a national hero. He was knighted and had the cost of his expedition paid for by parliament.

The mammoth journey from Elephant Island to South Georgia in the *James Caird* was not a feat of foolhardy endurance but a necessary part of the rescue of the men of an expedition that had gone wrong. In 1914 on a further expedition to the Antarctic Shackleton's ship, *The Endurance*, had been caught by pack-ice and finally crushed and sunk. *The James Caird* was one of its boats. Shackleton led his men in three such small boats across ice-floes to a camp on Elephant Island. His daring trip with his five companions was the only hope of rescue for the rest of the members of the expedition. Even when they reached South Georgia they had to cross huge glaciers, some of them 10 000 feet high to get to the Norwegian fishing-station at Stromness. The men left behind on Elephant Island were finally rescued only after four attempts.

Shackleton's daring and heroism endeared him to the public and his 1921 Antarctic expedition created a great deal of interest. It was cut short by his sudden death of *angina pectoris* at Grytviken in South Georgia on 5 January 1922. He was buried there—a fitting resting-place for such a man. Shackleton's expeditions were noted as much for the scientific information obtained as for the courage and endurance of the leader.

THE DEVIL'S DISCIPLE

George Bernard Shaw (1856-1950)

Outside the National Gallery in Merrion Square there are two statues, one of William Dargan,* the founder, and the other of Ireland's most famous playwright who regarded the pictures in the gallery as an important part of his education. When he died a rich man he left one third of his estate to the trustees. Bernard Shaw, or GBS but never "George" which he hated, was born in Synge Street, Dublin on 26 July 1856, the son of an unsuccessful merchant and a mother who was a dynamic teacher of music. Her teacher, George Vandeleur Lee became a kind of second father to

Shaw. Lee and Mrs Shaw left for London and the talented son soon followed, determined to be a writer. For many years he had no success; five novels were flops but in time he became one of the funniest and most trenchant critics of music and theatre in the country. He joined the Fabian society which attempted to reform society constitutionally and overcame great shyness to become an effective public speaker. He began writing plays, strongly influenced by Ibsen, which dealt with rather more serious themes than Edwardian playgoers were used to and which were written with remarkable wit. Such plays as *Arms and the Man* (1894), *Candida* (1894), *The Devil's Disciple* (1896), *Heartbreak House* (1920) and *St Joan* (1927) made him in time world famous and his comedy *Pygmalion* (1912) had a second life as the highly successful musical *My Fair Lady* (1956). His reputation as a wit and mocking critic of society made his name well-known to many who had never seen his plays. GBS was also famous for his advocacy of vegetarianism, rational clothing and spelling reform. He wrote more than fifty plays which, when published, had long, brilliantly written introductions. He died on 2 November 1950 aged ninety-four. He claimed (how seriously no one can tell, for his Irish sense of humour confused the British) that he was a better dramatist than Shakespear (as he insisted the name should be spelled.)

THE IRISH COUSINS

Edith Somerville (1858-1949)
Violet Martin (1862-1915)

The bewildered figure of Major Yeates battling with Mrs
"Kaydogawn" and outwitted at every turn by Flurry Knox
and Slipper has become very well known to the TV
audience after the recent filming of *The Irish RM*. Those who
knew the stories before the series was made were a little bit
disappointed. Since the three RM books were written (in
1899, 1905 and 1915) they have remained popular and
usually in print. Somehow the descriptions of ghosts,
horse-dealing and mishandled hunts were funnier as

stories than on the screen—it was the way they told them. The authors were cousins, both women in spite of the ambiguity of the names they used, E Œ Somerville and Martin Ross, and a rare example of effective literary collaboration. Edith was born on 2 May 1858 in the island of Corfu where her father, a Lt Colonel, was stationed, but from the age of one she lived in Drishane, Castletownshend, Co Cork, learning to become an expert horsewoman and a church organist. Violet was four years younger (born on 11 June 1862) and came from Ross House, near Moycullen in Co Galway. They met when Violet was twenty-four and began a partnership which continued for long after Violet's death on 21 December 1915. According to Edith, Violet's spirit filled her as she wrote the novel, *The Big House at Inver* (1927), which was published as being written by Somerville & Ross. They were notably different in temperament, Violet having the dark imagination (which led to many spooky touches in even their funniest stories) and the wilder humour; while the Irishness (including the Gaelic) and the knowledge of animals was Edith's. When the stories were written some people felt that condescending fun was being made of the Irish and the teleplays were not free of it, but on the whole they are accurate accounts of life in the Ireland of the time. Somerville and Ross's greatest novel was *The Real Charlotte* (1894). Edith was one of the people who spoke to Michael Collins* on the day he died. She lived to be ninety-one, dying at home in Drishane on 8 October 1949.

"THE SHOOK"

James Stephens (1825-1901)

If 1848 was the year of revolution, 1849 was the year of the political refugee. Only in France did revolution succeed and it was natural that the failed revolutionaries of the rest of Europe should look to Paris as a refuge. They thronged the narrow streets of the Quartier latin, living in poor lodging houses like the Pension Bannery on the rue Lacépède (where Balzac set *Père Goriot*). Among the residents was a young Irish refugee, James Stephens. He had been born in Kilkenny in 1825 and had become a railway engineer. He joined the Young Ireland movement and took part in the

Smith O'Brien rising of 1848. Wounded at a skirmish at Ballingarry, he narrowly escaped capture. In exile he attended lectures at the Sorbonne and worked for the *Moniteur Universel* newspaper, translating Dickens for the *feuilleton*. His interest in revolution was kept alive by encounters with refugee Italians and with Karl Marx who imbued him with socialist ideas and later enrolled him in the *International*, the association that sought to unite the working-classes of all countries for their economic emancipation). In 1856 he founded the Irish Republican Brotherhood (generally known as the Fenian Movement) which believed in using force to bring about an independent Irish republic. He called himself *An Seabhach* (The Hawk), which his Dublin followers rendered as "The Shook." With financial help from those Irish people who had settled in America after the Famine he set up a propaganda paper, *The Irish People*, and planned a rising for 1865. His secret organisation, of "circles" of 820 members controlled by "centres," was infiltrated by British intelligence and the "head centre," Stephens, was forced to flee to New York. From there he planned a rising for 1867 which was a fiasco. Afterwards he returned to Paris to live by journalism and teaching. A subscription raised by old Fenian friends enabled him to retire to Ireland in 1886. He remained a shadowy figure all his life, lacking the charisma of such men as O'Donovan Rossa and O'Mahony. He died in Blackrock on 21 April 1901.

DRACULA'S SECRETARY

Bram Stoker (1847-1912)

"The mouth, as far as I could see it under the heavy moustache, was fixed and rather cruel-looking, with peculiarly sharp white teeth; these protruded over the lips, whose remarkable ruddiness showed astonishing vitality in a man of his years." The description is of Count Dracula of Transylvania, the most famous vampire in literature—or is it? Might it not be that of Sir Henry Irving, the great actor-manager, whose personality was as strong off-stage as on? Bram (short for Abraham) Stoker was born in Fairview, Dublin in 1847, the son of a clerk at Dublin Castle. He was bookish and solitary as a child but became quite an athlete at Trinity. He joined the civil service but his passion was the theatre. He wrote unpaid drama reviews for the *Evening Mail* and gladly accepted the post of secretary to Irving, his hero, in 1876. He worked very hard and was alternately charmed by and appalled at his overpowering master. His classical horror-tale *Dracula* was published in 1897 and its main character owes something to that of Irving. It alone of a dozen novels has survived, though *The Lair of the White Worm* is still creepily readable. His first published work, *The Duties of Clerks of Petty Sessions in Ireland*, is now not read at all. Irving died in 1905 and after that Stoker seemed to lose heart. His last published book was *Personal Reminiscences of Henry Irving* (1906). He died in 1912, of exhaustion his friends said. His book *Dracula*, though not so fine a study of vampirism as his fellow-townsman Sheridan Le Fanu's *Carmilla* (1872), caught the world's imagination and the character of the sanguinary count passed from literature into folk-myth.

GULLIVER AMONG THE LILLIPUTIANS

Jonathan Swift (1667-1745)

"...a young healthy child well nursed is at a year old a most delicious, nourishing and wholesome food, whether stewed, roasted, baked or boiled..." So wrote one of the best stylists in English literature and a patriotic Irishman (born on 30 November 1667) who nevertheless swore that he hated "dirty Dublin and miserable Ireland." He even denied he was born there but there is no doubt that his place of birth was Hoey's Court not far from St Patrick's Cathedral, of which he later became the most famous dean. His university career at Trinity was undistinguished and he was graduated only by consent. He became the secretary of Sir William Temple of Moor Park. There he met Hester Johnson (whom he called Stella) and with whom he fell in love. The people of Dublin believed that they were married and it is true that she stayed in Ireland from the time of his appointment to the deanery until her death in 1728.

Swift's satirical proposal about eating babies was intended to sting the consciences of the English politicians who cared nothing for Ireland and who used the country merely to make profits for themselves. He understood well the minds of the exploiters because the reason for his hated exile was his satire of Whig politicians and the enmity of Queen Anne, who refused him a bishopric. He became an Irish patriot when he realised the appalling conditions of the poor in Ireland, especially those who lived near his deanery. His most famous book, *Gulliver's Travels* (1726), was both a satire on contemporary politics and a terrible vision of depraved and miserable mankind. By an irony which he would have appreciated, this bitter book has become a children's classic. Another woman, Esther Vanhomrigh, loved him and followed him to Ireland. Her persistent attentions and Swift's acceptance of them were the cause of a serious estrangement with Stella. Esther died in 1723 of tuberculosis but her last years were very unhappy because she felt that Swift had treated her cruelly. Swift himself was harried in his later years by the fear of madness. His physical symptoms were those of Meuniére's syndrome which causes nausea, vertigo and tinnitus— enough to make any man think he was going out of his mind. He died of chronic meningitis on 19 October 1745. His bleak opinion of mankind in general did not extend to individuals for he was a genial and faithful friend and a dispenser of judicious charity. And, in his own words, he

"Gave what little wealth he had / To build a house for fools and mad." This became St Patrick's Psychiatric Hospital in James's Street, Dublin. He is buried beside Stella in St Patrick's Cathedral close.

THE MEDITATIVE MAN

John Millington Synge (1871-1909)

On 24 March 1909 in the Elpis Clinic in Dublin there died of
lymphatic cancer a man of rich imagination and richer
language. He was John Synge, whom his friend W B Yeats*
called "that slow man / That meditative man..." Yeats took
the credit for directing him towards the artistic career that
suited his talents best, the rendering of the wilder spirit of
western Ireland into drama for Yeats's theatre, The Abbey.
He was born in Rathfarnham on 16 April 1871. He was
sickly as a child and soon rejected the strict evangelistic
religion of his family preferring instead to find his

spirituality in nature. He was a constant traveller who knew every road in Wicklow, and was, incidentally, acquainted with Wicklow's many tramps. He had thought of becoming a professional violinist and in his early manhood had written some of the morbid poetry that was then fashionable, but it was a meeting with Yeats in Paris that showed him his way. The young poet told the future playwright to go to the Aran Islands and "express a life that has never found expression." Four summer stays, mainly in Inis Mean, resulted in the book *The Aran Islands* and gave him the material for two of his famous plays, *Riders to the Sea* (1904) and *The Playboy of the Western World* (1907). He helped manage the theatre and contributed three other important plays: *The Shadow of the Glen* (1903), *The Tinker's Wedding* (1907) and *Deirdre of the Sorrows* (unfinished at his death). He fell in love with Molly Allgood*, the actress who had played Pegeen Mike in *The Playboy*, and wrote *Deirdre* in her honour. His rage for life and the hard regimen he imposed upon his body were an instinctive response to a sense that he would be short-lived. He foretold this end in a poem, "To the Oaks of Glencree":

> *There'll come a season when you'll stretch*
> *Black boards to cover me:*
> *Then in Mount Jerome I will lie, poor wretch,*
> *With worms eternally.*

His works were once thought wild and shocking but now are properly appreciated as the finest of the Abbey plays.

THE WORKER SAINT

Matt Talbot (1856-1925)

At the south end of the river Liffey in Dublin there is a limestone sculpture of Matt Talbot beside the new bridge named after him. The figure carries a heavy load but from the side seems to be emerging from the solid stone. It seems quite appropriate for the character. He was born on 2 May 1856, one of a family of twelve from Aldborough court in the poor north city. He had to leave school at the age of twelve to work as a messenger-boy in a bottling firm. There he developed a taste for alcohol which left him penniless even when he was earning the salary of an adult labourer. Then out of the seeming wreck of a man something emerged. At the age of twenty-seven he pledged himself to give up drink. He went to mass every day before work, to St Francis Xavier's church in Gardiner Street, and many times on a Sunday to different churches around the city. Workmates at Martin's timberyard on the North Wall noticed how little he ate and his mother discovered that he slept on bare boards. He averted his eyes from newspapers and hoardings but recommended friends to read Louis-Marie de Montfort and the Spanish mystic Maria d'Agreda. When he died in Granby Lane on 7 June 1925 on the way to St Saviour's church he was discovered to be wearing chains under his clothes. Our anti-heroic age does not know what to make of such a holy man and finds him an embarrassment. Our great-grandparents who were his contemporaries found such uncompromising faith quite natural.

THE FIRST REPUBLICAN

Theobald Wolfe Tone (1763-98)

In the 1790s Paris was the most interesting and exciting city in the world. Young emigré revolutionaries from every country in Europe gathered there to marvel at people bold enough to execute their king for treason. They competed fiercely for French help to overthrow unpopular regimes in their own countries. Few were as successful as the young Irishman, Wolfe Tone, who within a year of his arrival in Paris had convinced Carnot, the Minister of Public Safety, of the efficacy of an invasion of Ireland. So in 1796 forty-three ships and 15 000 men under Lazare Hoche, with Tone by his side, sailed to invade Ireland, overthrow the British government there and set up a republic.

What made Tone so successful was his marvellous ability to express himself clearly and to persuade people that he was right. He was born in Dublin on 20 June 1763 but though he was called to the bar in 1789 he had little taste for law and preferred politics. As early as 1791 he had written *An Argument on Behalf of the Catholics of Ireland*, a pamphlet which won over many Irish Protestants to the belief that their fellow-countrymen must be given political rights. Not long afterwards he helped form the United Irishmen to campaign for a more democratic government. His charm helped smooth relations between the Belfast and Dublin branches of the society. When it was suppressed by the government he won over the more timid to the idea of seeking French aid in the setting up of a republic.

At the end Tone failed to achieve his aims but it was not entirely his fault. He cannot be blamed for the gale which scattered the 1796 invasion nor for the fact that the United Irishmen were disorganised when a second invasion attempt came from France in 1798. Captured after the failure of that invasion and the Rising of 1798, he took his own life and died on 19 November 1798. At his grave at Bodenstown many different groups gather every year to commemorate his life. Through his beautifully written *Journal* he continues to have an influence over his countrymen who have found it possible "to break the connection with England" but much more difficult "to substitute the common name of Irishman in place of the denominations of Protestant, Catholic and Dissenter."

THE GREAT FRANCISCAN

Luke Wadding (1588-1657)

The history of the Catholic Church in Ireland from the Reformation to Catholic Emancipation is like a wave-curve with depressing troughs (as in the Penal days) and quite remarkable highs. One of these highs was the Franciscanising of the country that occurred in the first half of the seventeenth century. In 1612 there were only eight friaries in Ireland but by 1630 there were forty-seven. It was the friars who helped to preserve the endangered Irish culture. During these same years Irish Franciscan colleges were established in Leuven (Louvain), Rome and Prague. The main guiding influence in this monumental work was a Waterford man, Luke Wadding, who was born in 1588 and died in Rome in 1657.

He was ordained in Spain in 1613 and given as his life's work the task of writing the history of his order. The composition of *Annales Ordinis Minorum* in eight volumes took from 1625 to 1654 but during this period Wadding also edited the works of his great Irish Franciscan predecessor, Duns Scotus, in sixteen volumes. He encouraged the writing of the *Annals of the Four Masters* at Leuven and did what he could to get the Catholic monarchs of Europe to intervene on behalf of their co-religionists in Ireland during the Cromwellian wars. However he was unsuccessful and Cromwell's soldiers destroyed most of the monastic houses and put their occupants to the sword.

THE SIEGE GOVERNOR

George Walker (c. 1646-90)

In Derry, about halfway up the perimeter west wall (Derry's seventeenth century walls are famous) there was, until it was blown up on the night of 28 August 1973, a tall column with the figure of a clergyman on top. In his left hand he held a bible and with arm outstretched his right finger pointed to a spot beyond Ross's Bay where the River Foyle narrows again. The monument was completed on August 12, exactly 139 years after the character's finest hour. For the statue was that of the Rev George Walker and he pointed to the place where the ship Mountjoy broke the blockading boom and lifted the Siege of Derry on July 18, 1689 (old calendar). He is the most famous character of the siege which lasted for 238 days and helped establish William III on the throne of England, mainly because he wrote the story that most people remember.

He was born about 1646 in England where his father, also a Rev George, a fact confusing to many biographers, had fled in 1641 to escape the effects of the Catholic insurrection. He graduated from TCD and in 1674 became rector of Donoughmore, Co Tyrone. There, to counter the forces of James II, he raised the Charlemont regiment and as its major brought the soldiers to the fortified city of Derry in late 1688 to hold it for Dutch William. He was made governor of the besieged city in April, 1689 and claimed in his book on the siege that he took part in any fighting there was. When the broken boom signalled the end of the siege he was sent to London to ask for money to restore the ruined city. He was fêted as the hero of Derry, given £5,000 for his personal use (a fortune in those days) but nothing for the city. He apparently developed a taste for the military life for he was with the king at the Battle of the Boyne and was killed by a stray ball on 1 July 1690.

THE RUINED BUTTERFLY

Oscar Wilde (1854-1900)

In 1895 fashionable London flocked to the St James's Theatre to see the latest and wittiest of Mr Wilde's agreeable comedies, *The Importance of Being Earnest*. The most famous wit in London, the dazzler of the Café Royale, had reached the heights. The sophisticates of the metropolis acknowledged him their master, and the career of self-advertisement was no longer necessary. Yet as a brilliant classical scholar Wilde should have known enough about Greek tragedy to realise that arrogance is followed by downfall and even then the Furies were waiting in the wings to claim him. In five years he was dead, an

215

impoverished and lonely exile, after suffering public disgrace, bankruptcy, and a two-year prison sentence.

Oscar Fingal O'Flahertie Wills Wilde was born in Dublin on 16 October 1854, the son of Sir William Wilde, an eye and ear specialist, as famous for his *amours* as for his skill with the knife, and Jane Francesca Elgee who wrote nationalist poetry for *The Nation* as "Speranza." He had a brilliant career at Trinity and afterwards at Magdalen College, Oxford. He was one of the founders of the Aesthetic movement which held that art was sufficient licence for any behaviour however extreme. He worked mainly as a journalist and after marriage to Constance Lloyd became editor of *The Woman's World*. His poetry was too precious to be popular and his main artistic reputation was as a café wit; yet he wrote some tender and charming fairy stories for children. Towards the end of the nineties he wrote the four comedies for which he is still famous: *Lady Windermere's Fan* (1892), *A Woman of No Importance* (1893), *An Ideal Husband* (1893) and *The Importance of Being Earnest*.

In 1891 Wilde formed a friendship with Lord Alfred Douglas, the son of the Marquess of Queensbury. They were assumed to be lovers and after this fact became public during a libel case brought by Wilde against Queensbury, Wilde was sentenced to two years hard labour for homosexual acts which were then criminal offences. He suffered greatly from humiliation and hardship in prison and when he was released in 1897 he wrote his finest poem, "The Ballad of Reading Gaol." He lived for some time in Italy and France but died in Paris of syphilis and cerebral meningitis on 30 November 1900 and was buried in Père Lachaise cemetery. Wilde was greatly talented and intolerant, disdainful of public opinion and finally crucified by it.

PEG OF OLD DRURY

Margaret Woffington (?1714-60)

On 3 May 1757, at the end of a performance of *As You Like It*, the actress playing Rosalind (one of the best ever to play that male-costume part) was speaking the epilogue. She had, as usual, charmed the rowdy audience with her performance and when she reached the confusing lines that always cause the men in the audience to beam with pleasure, "If I were a woman I would kiss as many of you as had beards that pleased me," she faltered, staggered off stage and collapsed. It was the end of the stage career of one of the best actresses ever and one who specialised in that

217

unconvincing but attractive example of stage transvestism, the "breeches part." She was born on 18 October, probably in the year 1714, the daughter of a bricklayer and a laundress. She took to acting early and by 1737 was playing the part of Ophelia in a Smock Alley production of *Hamlet*. In those years Dublin's theatre was as prominent as London's and when Woffington appeared in the Theatre Royal, Drury Lane, it was as a star. She gave her most famous "breeches" part, Sir Harry Wildair, in the play *The Constant Couple* which was written by the Derry-born George Farquhar. She took London by storm and for seventeen years she was the queen of the theatre in both capitals. She had many lovers, including the great David Garrick, and was known for her beauty and generosity. She had a temper too, and once chased a rival actress and wounded her with a dagger. The greatest tribute to her personality and popularity was her election to the all-male Dublin "Beefsteak Club." She died on 28 March 1760, three years after her collapse on stage, but not before she had set up a pension fund for her mother and younger sister and endowed almshouses at Teddington on the Thames where there is still a memorial to her.

THE SINGING MASTER

William Butler Yeats (1865-1939)

On a cloudy day in September 1948 the corvette L E *Macha* steamed into Galway Bay. The remains of Ireland's greatest modern poet had come home to be buried where he had stated he wished to lie, under bare Ben Bulben's head in Drumcliffe churchyard. It was countryside he loved: where he had roamed as a boy, learned to fish and begun to understand the old spirit of Gaelic Ireland. William Butler Yeats was born in Dublin on 13 June 1865, the eldest of four children of John Butler Yeats, the nationalist portraitist who "charged too little for his paintings." His mother's people, the Pollexfens, were Sligo millers and it was to Sligo and Leitrim that he turned when trying to find a poetic voice. The young Yeats was strongly influenced towards nationalism by his father and by an old Fenian, John O'Leary. He wrote plays and poetry based upon the old Celtic legends. In 1889 he met Maud Gonne, the daughter of an English officer, who had become committed to Irish nationhood, and his protracted and often frustrating love affair with her was the source of much unhappiness and strong literary inspiration. Under her influence he became a member of the Irish Republican Brotherhood and took an active part in the centenary celebrations of the 1798 rising. About this time his friendship with Lady Gregory* and Edward Martyn led to the founding of the Abbey Theatre and the writing of generally untheatrical plays. The 1916 Rising affected him deeply and he determined to make his home in Ireland. After 1919 Yeats and his wife Georgie lived at Thoor Ballylee, a converted Norman keep, a life "serene and full of order." In 1923 he received the Nobel prize for literature and served as a senator in the newly established Irish Free State. A meagre income from writing was supplemented by more lucrative lecture-tours. Winters from 1927 on were spent in France and Italy for health reasons. Yeats died at Roquebrune near Monaco on 28 January 1939. He was a great if idiosyncratic interpreter of himself and his country.

The Poolbeg Book of Irish Placenames
by
Sean McMahon

Dinnseanchas, the lore of placenames, is a fascinating study and a great hobby for the do-it-yourselfenthusiast. This collection contains a province-by-province, county-by-county guide with a a useful introduction ahd glossary

POOLBEG

The Poolbeg Golden Treasury of Well Loved Poems

Edited by Sean McMahon

By the compiler of *Rich and Rare*
and
The Poolbeg Book of Children's Verse

A delightful anthology of everyone's favourite poems, from Shakespeare to Patrick Kavanagh

POOLBEG

Destiny of Dreams

by
Michael Bowler

A boy grows up in Cahirciveen with dreams of
freedom but has to face the realities of life in
Ireland in the 1950s.

A brilliant first novel: evocative, lyrical and
passionate

POOLBEG

Women Surviving
Studies in the History of Irish Women in the 19th and 20th centuries

Edited by

Maria Luddy and Cliona Murphy

This highly original collection of historical articles addresses aspects of women's history in nineteenth and early twentieth-century Ireland, including: nuns in society; paupers and prostitutes; the impact of international feminists on the Irish suffrage movement and women's contribution to post-Independence Irish politics.

POOLBEG